THE ECONOMICS
OF WORK AND PAY

Harper & Row, Publishers
New York, Evanston, San Francisco, London

THE ECONOMICS OF WORK AND PAY

Albert Rees

Princeton University

CONTENTS

INTRODUCTION

This is a book about labor economics, which is the branch of economic analysis dealing with such topics as the supply of labor, the allocation of labor among uses, the extent and incidence of unemployment, and the determination of wages. Two questions will help us define the field. First, why is labor economics a separate branch of economics? Second, how does labor economics differ from industrial relations?

The answer to the first question is that labor markets are very different from commodity markets and from markets for other factors of production. The employment of labor involves a continuing personal relationship between an employer and an employee, whereas transactions in most other markets are by comparison brief and impersonal. Labor economics also involves the study of a major economic institution—the trade union—that is very different from the firm and whose behavior is not covered by the main body of economic theory.

Industrial relations has as its main focus the relation between an employer and his workers or their union in a particular establishment or firm, while labor economics deals with larger aggregates. Because of its focus on smaller units, industrial relations is an interdisciplinary field that includes inputs from sociology, psychology, law, and personnel management as well as from economics. For much the same reason, industrial relations is largely an applied field concerned with practice and the training of practitioners rather than with theory and measurement. It is thus related to the basic social sciences, including economics, as engineering is to the physical sciences or medicine is to the biological sciences.

This book does not pretend to cover industrial relations, though clearly no hard and fast line can be drawn to separate the fields. Rather it will concentrate on the application of economic theory and statistics to the problems of labor markets.

The dominant tradition of labor economics in the United States up to the end of World War II was an institutionalist tradition based on the work of such scholars as Commons, Perlman, and Hoxie, whose intellectual roots lay in the law and a sociological rather than an economic theory. Economists trained in this tradition have tended to move into industrial relations as an institutional field. They developed closer ties with the other professions that contribute to industrial relations and became somewhat isolated from the main stream of economics.

In the past ten to fifteen years, a new and active interest in labor economics has grown up among scholars interested in applying the tools of economic theory to labor problems. The key figures in this analytical approach to labor economics have been H. Gregg Lewis, Melvin Reder, Gary Becker, William Bowen, and Jacob Mincer. Most of the work of these economists and their students has been published in journal articles and specialized monographs. Only very recently have there been attempts to survey and integrate this now rich and extensive literature. This book is one such attempt.

The first draft of this book was written in London during 1969–1970 at the National Board for Prices and Incomes. I would like to express my deep appreciation to the Board and particularly to its Chairman, Mr. Aubrey Jones, and its Joint Deputy Chairman, Mr. Ralph Turvey, for allowing me to use the Board's facilities and to participate to some extent in its work. I hope that the insights into British labor problems that I gained in this period have helped to broaden my work. I am also deeply grateful to the John Simon Guggenheim Memorial Foundation and to Princeton University for grants that permitted me to spend a full year in study and writing.

The first draft of the book was read in whole or in part by my colleagues William G. Bowen, T. Aldrich Finegan, Daniel S. Hamermesh, and Michael K. Taussig. It has been much improved by their suggestions.

Finally, I would like to thank the Industrial Relations Section, Princeton University, for its support throughout the enterprise, and in particular Miss Karen Stout for her careful typing of the manuscript.

Needless to say, none of the people or organizations whose help is mentioned above is in any way responsible for my conclusions or my errors.

ALBERT REES

THE ECONOMICS
OF WORK AND PAY

PART I

The Supply of Labor

Labor-Force Participation

THE MEANING OF LABOR SUPPLY

In the writings of the classical economists, discussion of labor supply concerned the forces that determine the size of the population of working age and, especially, the effect of changes in real wages on the growth of this population. Not much was said about the amount of work supplied by a population of any given size. More recent practice in labor economics reverses this emphasis. Demography has become a separate discipline, or at least a separate branch of economics or of sociology, with well-developed methods of its own and with the study of the growth of population as its primary concern. Labor economists now define the supply of labor as the amount of work supplied by a given population. I shall follow recent precedent and treat the size of the population as exogenous.

The amount of labor supplied by a given population depends on four factors. The first is the *labor-force participation rate*, or

3

the fraction of the population engaged in or seeking gainful employment. This has been the subject of much recent research, which will be reviewed in this chapter. The second is the *number of hours* people are willing to work per week or per year while they are in the labor force. This somewhat neglected aspect of labor supply is treated in Chapter 2. A third factor, still more neglected, is the *amount of effort* workers put forth while at work. This is discussed briefly in the last section of Chapter 2. The final factor is the *level of training and skill* that workers bring to their jobs. This has been an important topic in the recent literature and is the subject of Chapter 3.

THE DEFINITION
OF THE LABOR FORCE

The labor force is defined as the number of people who work for pay or profit or who are unemployed during any part of some short period of time, usually a week. In the United States as of 1972, the employed are defined as those who worked one hour or more for wages or salary during the reference week, or did 15 hours or more of unpaid work in a family business or farm. Those absent from work because of vacation, illness, bad weather, or industrial disputes are also counted as employed, but in the separate sub-category "with a job but not at work." The unemployed are those who are on layoff from a job or who have no job but have looked for work during the preceding four weeks and were available for work during the reference week. The labor force as defined in the United States is now limited to those 16 years of age and older; the small amount of labor supplied by those under 16 is not counted. Before 1967 the lower age limit for inclusion in the labor force was 14 years.

Being in or out of the measured labor force is an all-or-nothing matter; every person in the civilian noninstitutional population 16 years of age and over is assigned to one category or the other in the decennial censuses or is estimated to be in one or the other through monthly sample surveys at other times. The labor-force participation rate of any category of the population by age, sex, color, or marital status is the number of persons in that category who are in the labor force divided by the whole number in that category.

TABLE 1

Labor-Force Participation Rates by Age and Sex, 1971

Age	Male	Female
16 and 17	47.3	34.3
18 and 19	69.3	53.2
20–24	85.7	57.8
25–34	96.2	45.5
35–44	96.6	51.6
45–54	93.9	54.3
55–64	82.2	42.9
65 and over	25.5	9.5
All ages, 16 and over	80.0	43.4

Source: *Manpower Report of the President,* March 1972, Table A-2.

Labor-force participation rates by age and sex for a recent year are shown in Table 1. Large variations in rates among the groups are immediately apparent. The participation rate is generally higher for men than for women, but within each sex there is substantial variation by age, and the age patterns for men and women are highly dissimilar. To explain these patterns of participation we must look at how decisions about the use of time are made within the household.

LABOR-SUPPLY DECISIONS
WITHIN THE HOUSEHOLD

Until very recently the formal theory of labor supply concerned the choices between labor and leisure made by one individual. This theory is reviewed in Chapter 2 in connection with hours of work. In the last few years, however, labor-supply theory has been set in a broader framework, which is outlined in this section in a less technical way.

The concept of the labor force separates market work from all other uses of time, including education and work within the household. It is therefore an oversimplification to view decisions on whether or not to be in the labor force as a choice between work and leisure, where leisure includes only recreation and time for such personal needs as eating and sleeping. Most of the men and single women under age 25 who are not in the labor force are full-time students, and going to school or college is certainly not leisure. Most married women not in the labor force are full-time housekeepers for their own families, and keeping house is hard work. Only among the elderly is leisure the chief alternative to work, since most people over 65 who are not in the labor force are retired. At all ages, but especially among the elderly, some of those not in the labor force are physically unable to work.

Since most people live in families or households rather than as single individuals, decisions about who is and who is not in the labor force, as well as the related decision about how many hours of work they would like to supply, are best viewed as decisions about how the household divides its total available time between market work and nonmarket activities.[1] Whether the members of the household make these decisions collectively or individually or whether the head makes them for the whole household need not concern us here. Presumably there are households that make their decisions in each of these ways, but the nature of decision making within households is not usually considered to be within the realm of economics.

Decisions about the allocation of time will reflect the total resources of the household, of which the most important are the time of household members of working age and the household's income from sources other than work. These decisions reflect also the opportunities for market work available to members of the household, including their potential market wage, their comparative advantages in nonmarket activities, and the amount and nature of household work that needs to be performed. An increase in the family's resources, unaccompanied by any other change in opportunities—such as an inheritance that substantially increases nonlabor income—should reduce total labor supply. Thus it might lead the family to decide that a teenage son should stay in school longer, that the elderly grandfather should retire earlier, or that the working wife should become a full-time homemaker. Underlying the expectation that a rise in nonlabor income tends to reduce participation in the labor force is the assumption that for at least some members of most households, more leisure or more of some other nonmarket activity is preferred to some portion of current market work, and that the higher nonlabor income will make it possible to engage in more of the preferred activity.

But this is not to say that there is such disutility attached to all work that in a household whose nonlabor income was very high no one would work.

A rise in the wage for the market work open to some members of the household may induce more participation by these members. Thus a rise in the salaries of schoolteachers (relative to other wages and prices) should induce some women who have left work to care for their families to return to teaching. They could use some combination of hired domestic help, purchased services, and the reallocation of household duties to other members of the family to make up for the loss of some of their time in the home, or the family could consume somewhat less of the "goods" produced by work in the home, such as a tidy kitchen, home cooking, or a well-kept garden, and instead could consume more market goods.

This case is somewhat more complicated than the previous one, since it involves both a change in relative prices (which produces a substitution effect because it makes work more attractive) and a change in total resources (which produces an income effect because it leaves the family better off). For those families that include a teacher already at work full time, the sole effect is to increase family income, which might tend to reduce the labor-force participation rates of others in the family. To assume that the net effect of the wage change for all families taken together is to increase participation rates is to assume that the substitution effect on balance outweighs the income effect.

The values attached to other nonmarket alternatives also affect the household's decisions. If either the wife or the teenage son must work to maintain the family's customary living standard, and if both could earn the same market wage, then the extent to which the son's additional schooling would augment his earnings in the future must be weighed against the costs of the wife's absence from the home now. The birth of a child will increase the amount of household work to be performed by the mother, by some other members of the family, or by someone hired to care for the child. Whether or not this will cause the wife to leave the labor force will depend in part on how the family values alternative arrangements for child care.

None of this is intended to suggest that the allocation of resources within the household is governed entirely by economic forces. Far from it. Heavy weight must be given to tradition and to concepts of appropriate social roles. There must be many house-holds in which the wife's earning power exceeds the husband's and the husband would be an adequate housekeeper. Yet the reversal of customary roles that makes the wife the breadwinner and the husband the housekeeper is extremely rare in the United States. It is found largely in places where employment oppor-tunities for men have become so scarce that unemployed men cannot hope to find steady work while women can (in some de-pressed mining communities where low-wage manufacturing jobs for women are available, for example). The largest adjustment that has been permitted until now by usual concepts of male dignity is for both husband and wife to work and for the wife to hire household help from her earnings.

PARTICIPATION RATES
BY AGE, SEX, AND COLOR

This section reviews briefly some research findings on the labor-force participation of particular demographic groups. The ques-tion of the relation of participation rates to the unemployment rate—that is, to the strength of the demand for labor—will be saved for separate consideration in the following section.

If a household includes an able-bodied male head who has com-pleted his formal education and not yet reached the age of retire-ment, it is taken for granted in our society that he will be a member of the labor force. In the census week of 1960 the labor-force participation rate of married men (with wife present) between the ages of 25 and 54 was 97.6 percent.[2] Presumably most of the remaining 2.4 percent were disabled. Even a married man with enough income from property to escape the necessity of working would undoubtedly have reported himself as employed in the management of his own investments.

Although the labor-force participation rate of married men in the prime age groups is very high, it is still possible to find and explain differences in the rates for different population categories. For example, Bowen and Finegan report that the participation rate is lower for nonwhites than for whites, and that for both groups it rises with the number of years of school completed. Both of these effects correspond to differences in market wages, which are higher for whites than for nonwhites and rise with education in both groups.

The compulsion of the social role of breadwinner does not have as much force for the unmarried man as it has for the married man. In the census week of 1960 labor-force participation for men between the ages of 25 and 54 who were widowed, divorced, separated, or never married ranged from 79.1 to 84.3 percent, and the difference between the rates for these groups and rates for married men living with their wives is present in each of six narrower age ranges considered separately.[3] As Bowen and Finegan point out in their very careful analysis of this group, the data do not necessarily imply that being single causes a lower rate of participation. Rather the same underlying factors that led some single men to drop out of the labor force (such as lack of education, poor health, or low intelligence) might have contributed also to their failure to marry or to the dissolution of their marriages.

The 16 to 21 percent of those men not living with spouses who in any one week are not in the labor force are not all permanently out of it. These figures no doubt reflect the behavior of a larger fraction of the total population of single men, whose freedom from family responsibilities permits an alternation of periods of work with periods of nonmarket activities of one kind or another.

The positive relation between schooling and labor-force participation is also very strong for married women. This relation reflects, first of all, the higher reward of market work for educated workers and therefore the greater cost to them of nonmarket activities. Beyond this there is probably a positive correlation between the taste for schooling and the taste for market work, both of which involve a kind of discipline by others that is not present in work in one's own household. The girl who leaves school at the first opportunity may later prefer doing her family's cleaning and cooking to typing letters or assembling radios. Finally, the educated worker has access to more interesting and challenging kinds of jobs.

The labor-force participation of married women has been analyzed more intensively than that of other population groups. The principal early finding, from cross-sectional analysis by cities, was that the higher the earnings of males in a city, the lower the labor-force participation rate of women.[4] If male earnings and female earnings are not highly correlated (that is, if high male earnings do not imply high female earnings), male earnings will affect the participation of wives in much the same way as nonlabor income would, and the negative relation produced by the income effect is to be expected. By 1950, however, the correlation by city between male and female earnings was high enough to obscure the simple negative relation observed earlier.[5] This relation reemerges when male and female earnings are entered into the analysis as separate variables; the first then has the expected negative sign of an income effect; the second has the expected positive sign reflecting better opportunities for market work.[6] The study of married women in the labor force has also shown that the presence of children in the household, especially children of preschool age, has a strong inhibiting effect on market work. It is this effect that gives the two-humped appearance to the age profile of female participation rates shown in Table 1. The first peak is made up largely of young women who have not yet had their first child; the second consists largely of women whose youngest child has entered school.

The secular trend of labor-force participation of married women presents an apparent contradiction with cross-section results. As we have seen, the latter show a pronounced negative relation between wives' participation rates and husbands' incomes. Indeed, it is sometimes suggested that wives work only when their husbands' pay is inadequate, and that a living wage for men would permit many women to return to their preferred place in the home. However, as the average real income of male earners has risen gradually over the years, the participation rate of wives has also risen.[7] Evidently other forces also are at work.

The effect of two of these forces can be demonstrated readily. One is the increased schooling of women, which increases the value of their market work. To some extent this factor may work in reverse—that is, improved job opportunities for educated women encourage more women to continue their formal education. A second factor is the smaller average size of families. This means both that there are fewer children to care for and that the youngest child tends to be born when the mother is younger, which leaves more time for a career after the last child is in school. Other factors more difficult to quantify include the growth of occupations that employ women in pleasant surroundings, especially the clerical and sales occupations and teaching. Along with this has gone the shortening of standard hours of work, which makes it easier for a wife to have a full-time job and also to care for a house. New, improved, and cheaper products that reduce the amount of household work, such as washing machines, clothes dryers, and frozen foods, operate in the same direction. Whatever may have been the case in an earlier time, it now seems clear that many wives are in the labor force not from necessity, but by choice.

Labor-force participation rates of married women vary substantially across countries and among racial or ethnic groups within countries, reflecting differences in cultural attitudes toward the proper role of wives and differences in market opportunities. In the United States in 1960 the labor-force participation rate of urban black married women aged 14–54 was 47 percent, as compared with 35 percent for whites. Adjustment for the effects of such factors as schooling, age, and the presence of children reduces the gap from 12 percentage points to 7, but this is still substantial.[8] The remaining difference could be put down simply to culture, but it is possible to go somewhat beyond this. Glen Cain has pointed out three more specific factors.[9] First, black women, on average, work fewer hours per week than white women, probably because many are employed as part-time domestic servants. The difference in the amount of labor supplied by the two groups is therefore less than is suggested by the participation rates. Second, black families face discrimination in the housing market that is probably even greater than the discrimination against black women in the labor market. The result is that many black homes are unavoidably crowded, inducing a shift of consumption away from home goods and toward market goods that are bought with wage income. The final factor is the greater marital instability of black families, which could lead black wives to keep their ties to the labor force as subconscious insurance against the possibility of separation or divorce, and inadequate financial support from the former husband.

Labor-force participation in the ages from 16 to 24 is strongly influenced by decisions about the age at which a youth leaves school. An improvement in labor market conditions (rising wages and falling unemployment rates) raises the cost of staying in school and induces some students to leave school for work. But even among those who are still in school, there is substantial participation on a part-time and part-year basis (after school, on weekends, and during vacations). One might expect a negative relation between family income and the participation rates of students, with the students from more affluent families better able to afford to devote full time to their studies. But data for 1960 for urban male students 14–17 do not support such a view. Rather they show a participation rate for students from upper middle-income families as high as that for low-income families, even after adjustment for a variety of other variables.[10] One possible explanation is that the first jobs of teenagers are often arranged by their parents,. since teenagers have not yet established reputations of their own, and the prosperous parent has more and better connections with employers.

The trend of full-time participation by teenagers, especially those under 18, has been downward because of the gradual rise in the age of leaving school. At the opposite end of the life cycle, there has been a downward trend in the labor-force participation of older males, reflecting earlier ages of retirement. One basic factor in earlier retirement is the declining importance of self-employment, which permits a gradual tapering off of work rather than a sudden ending. Participation rates now drop abruptly at age 65, reflecting the compulsory retirement policies of most employers and the availability of full rights to pensions and social security benefits. Even before age 65, however, participation rates begin to decline. This decline has been encouraged by the availability of partial social security benefits and some early pension rights. Some of those who retire early may lack the physical vigor to continue to work, especially in manual jobs. Some have lost their jobs because of plant shutdowns or technological change and have given up the search for new ones.

The general positive relation between schooling and participation is also present among older persons. For urban males aged 55–64, Bowen and Finegan report participation rates of less than 80 percent for those who completed fewer than 8 years of school and of more than 90 percent for college graduates.[11] A major source of this difference must be that college graduates have more varied and interesting work, from which they are less eager to retire. They are close to the peak of their earning power after age 55, while the earnings of those with little education are more dependent on physical strength and stamina and are therefore more likely to have declined.

Combining all demographic groups, including those not mentioned separately above, the labor-force participation rate of persons 14 years old and over has been remarkably constant in the United States since 1900, at about 55 percent of the population. This constancy has been produced by two offsetting trends: first, a fall in the male participation rate because of prolonged schooling and earlier retirement, and second, a substantial rise in the female participation rate. In the first six decades of this century the fraction of the labor force made up of males fell from more than four-fifths to about two-thirds. The offsetting rise in female participation occurred entirely among married women.[12]

THE EFFECT
OF CHANGES IN DEMAND

We now turn to the effect of variations in the strength of the demand for labor as a force affecting the measured participation rate. Discussion of this topic began in the 1930s with the emergence of the so-called *added-worker hypothesis.* This view held that when the usual breadwinner was unemployed and seeking work, additional members of the household would enter the labor force in an effort to maintain the family income; thus labor-force participation rates would rise as unemployment rose. At the time this argument was first made, unemployment was measured as a residual by estimating the trend of the labor force and subtracting an estimate of employment from it. The added-worker hypothesis, which argued that during a depression the labor force would be above the long-term trend, therefore implied that unemployment was being underestimated. At the present time, when the unemployed are counted directly, the added-worker hypothesis implies that unemployment is overestimated.

The contrary view, which has come to be called the *discouraged-worker hypothesis,* is that looking for work in conditions of general unemployment becomes so disheartening that some of the unemployed give up and withdraw from the labor force, and some people who would ordinarily enter the labor force do not do so. The size of the labor force therefore varies in the same direction as demand rather than in the opposite direction. When unemployment is measured by direct enumeration, as it has been since 1940, it is the discouraged-worker hypothesis that implies that unemployment is underestimated. It implies that we should add to those enumerated as unemployed another group, the *hidden unemployed*, who would be looking for work if they did not regard the search as hopeless.

Clearly both the added-worker and the discouraged-worker effects can be present at once for different households, so that the question to be decided by the evidence is which effect predominates, on balance. Mincer has shown that there is indeed increased labor-force participation of wives in those families where the husband has been unemployed.[13] However, the evidence from both cross-section and time-series data is clear that for all households taken together the discouragement effect is stronger. It seems reasonable that this should be so, as the following example suggests. Imagine that the unemployment rate rises from 4 to 6 percent—a substantial rise. The added-worker effect would tend to operate in the 2 percent of households with a newly unemployed member, but the discouragement effect could operate in many of the remaining 98 percent of households.[14]

Table 2 shows Bowen and Finegan's estimates of the sensitivity of labor-force participation rates to unemployment for males and for married women as estimated from intercity regressions for 1960. An increase of one percentage point in the overall unemployment rate[15] causes more than a 1-percent decline in the participation rate for all groups except males between 20 and 54. Even these smaller sensitivities are estimated from regression coefficients with high levels of statistical significance. Negative sensitivities (not shown here) were also estimated from significant regression coefficients for five of eight groups of women not living with husbands. The table makes clear that responsiveness to demand conditions is greatest in those population groups whose normal participation rates are low.

Somewhat similar results have been obtained from time-series regressions, though there has been a good deal of controversy about the proper statistical methods to use in making time-series estimates. Although it has been persuasively argued that some published estimates of hidden unemployment from time-series data are too high, there is now general agreement about the direc-

TABLE 2

Estimated Sensitivity of Labor-Force Participation to Unemployment (from Intercity Regressions for Census Week of 1960)

| Males | | Married Women, Husband Present | |
Age Group	Sensitivity[a]	Age Group	Sensitivity[a]
16–17	−5.6	17–19	−5.3
18–19	−2.0	20–24	−3.1
20–24	−0.4	25–29	−3.6
25–34	−0.3	30–34	−2.8
35–44	−0.4	35–39	−3.1
45–54	−0.6	40–44	−2.7
55–64	−1.5	45–54	−2.8
65 and over	−4.4	55–64	−3.6
		65 and over	−3.5

[a] The estimated sensitivity is the percentage change in the labor-force participation rate associated with a change of one percentage point in the overall unemployment rate.

Source: William G. Bowen and T. Aldrich Finegan, *The Economics of Labor Force Participation*, portions of Table 15-1, p. 482. Copyright © 1969 by Princeton University Press. Reprinted by permission of Princeton University Press.

tion of the effect, which is that labor-force participation varies in the same direction as demand. Table 3 shows Bowen and Finegan's estimates for the period 1954 (4) to 1965 (3), where the number in parentheses is the calendar quarter. These estimates are in general smaller than those from cross-section regressions. The authors warn against attaching too much meaning to the precise numbers, since they are highly sensitive to the period chosen for analysis. The estimates come from a model that expresses the labor-force participation rate for each group as a function of the unemployment rate, the ratio of manufacturing employment to total employment, and a quadratic time trend. The regression coefficients shown in Table 3 give the change in the labor-force participation rate (in percentage points) that results from a one-percentage-point increase in the overall unemployment rate in the previous calendar quarter, after adjusting for the indirect effects of this change in the unemployment rate through its effect on the ratio of manufacturing to nonmanufacturing employment where this ratio appears in the regression. Although the signs of all the significant

TABLE 3

Time-Series Regression Coefficients for the Relation Between Labor-Force Participation Rates and the Unemployment Rate, 1954 (4) to 1965 (3)

Age Group	Males	Females
14–15	−0.66	−0.54
16–17	−1.61	−1.46
18–19	−0.84	−0.46
20–24	−0.41	−[a]
25–34	−[a]	−0.25
35–44	−[a]	−0.25
45–54	−[a]	−0.18
55–64	−[a]	−0.41
65 and over	−0.49	−0.20
All ages, 14 and over	−0.22	−0.30

[a] Regression coefficient for unemployment not significant at the 10-percent level.

Source: William G. Bowen and T. Aldrich Finegan, *The Economics of Labor Force Participation*, portions of Table 16-1, p. 513. Copyright © 1969 by Princeton University Press. Reprinted by permission of Princeton University Press.

coefficients are negative, there are only two cases—those of the 16- and 17-year-olds—where a 1-percentage-point change in the unemployment rate causes the participation rate to drop as much as 1 percentage point.

The results of the studies of the sensitivity of labor-force participation to the strength of demand can be fitted into the framework of decision making outlined earlier. The added-worker effect in the households where the head becomes unemployed reflects both the temporary reduction in the family's normal income and the reduced need for other members to work in the home while the head is available to do some household chores. If all families had large holdings of liquid assets or could borrow in perfect capital markets, a temporary reduction in earned income might have only negligible effects on labor-force participation. The family's usual standard of consumption could be maintained by drawing down assets or by borrowing. The typical working-class family, however, has only a small amount of liquid assets and limited ability to borrow. Rates of interest on cash loans to such families, when they are available, are typically 18 percent per year or higher. Unemployment insurance benefits, for those eligible to receive them, often cover as little as a third of the income loss. Under these conditions, an increase in labor-force participation of other family members is an important alternative means of adjustment to unemployment even when it is expected to be temporary. Further research has been undertaken recently on the relation between the balance-sheet position of families and labor-force participation.

For the families that do not include a newly unemployed member, a rise in unemployment represents a fall in the expected return to market work with no change in current income. The jobs still available are likely to be lower paid or less attractive than before, and they can be found, if at all, only after longer and more costly search. For some of those deciding whether to stay in school or to leave, or whether to remain full-time housekeepers or to seek employment, this will tip the scales in favor of the nonmarket activity. The elderly worker who loses his job when unemployment rates are high is also more likely to settle for early retirement than he would be if the chances of finding a suitable new position were better.

The people of working age not in the labor force of any moment make up a large potential labor supply. Some could not be drawn into employment under any circumstances because of physical disabilities or heavy domestic responsibilities. Others, especially those with recent work experience, are a ready reserve, many of whom will take employment with slight inducement. This inducement could be either a rise in the attractiveness of market work or the provision of a substitute for the more essential nonmarket activities (for example, improved day-care facilities for preschool children).

As we have seen, there are many possible sources of variation in labor-force participation rates, pulling in different directions. The historical constancy of the overall participation rate must therefore be regarded as the result of chance rather than of the working of any unchanging economic or demographic law.

NOTES

1. In the text the analysis of labor-force participation and hours of work follows the traditional approach of dividing activity into market work and all other activity, which can be called "leisure" for convenience. An alternative approach that gives greater generality at the cost of greater complexity has been developed

by Gary Becker; see his "A Theory of the Allocation of Time," *Economic Journal* **75** (September 1965), 493–517. Becker points out that both productive activities and consumption take time. He labels the things from which people derive satisfaction as *commodities*, produced by a combination of two inputs, time and market goods. Commodities can then be classified by whether they are relatively time intensive (walking in the park) or market-goods intensive (eating steak), and work can be viewed as a particular commodity that yields more market goods than it uses and sometimes involves more negative than positive direct satisfaction. The outcome of such events as a rise in wages can then be analyzed in terms of their effects on time-intensive and market-goods-intensive activities, rather than simply on the amount of labor and leisure.

Certain implications of this approach do not emerge from traditional theory. Consider, for example, the effect of a rise in wages offset (compensated) by a lump-sum tax. Traditional theory predicts that this would induce more labor-force participation or the supply of more hours of work, since the marginal value of work (or the "price of leisure") is increased and the income effect has been offset. Becker points out that this change in circumstances will encourage reductions in all time-intensive activity—that is, it will presumably lead to substitution of activities that use more market goods for such activites as walking in the park and weeding one's own garden. There can thus be wage-induced changes in the internal composition of leisure activities or nonmarket work as well as changes in the allocation of time between the two major categories.

2. W. G. Bowen and T. A. Finegan, *The Economics of Labor Force Participation* (Princeton, N.J.: Princeton University Press, 1969), Table 3-2, p. 45. The present chapter relies heavily on Bowen and Finegan's comprehensive study.

3. *Ibid.*

4. See Erika H. Schoenberg and Paul H. Douglas, "Studies in the Supply Curve of Labor," *Journal of Political Economy* **45** (1937), 45–70; and Clarence D. Long, *The Labor Force Under Changing Income and Employment* (Princeton, N.J.: Princeton University Press, 1958), pp. 54–81. These studies analyze participation rates for both sexes, but the results for women have received the most attention from later writers.

5. Long, p. 59.

6. Jacob Mincer, "Labor Force Participation of Married Women," in *Aspects of Labor Economics*. A conference of the Universities—National Bureau Committee on Economic Research (Princeton, N.J.: Princeton University Press, 1962).

7. From 1948 to 1965 the rate for married women aged 14 to 64 rose 14 percentage points. See Bowen and Finegan, p. 206.

8. *Ibid*, p. 90.

9. Glen G. Cain, *Married Women in the Labor Force: An Economic Analysis* (Chicago: University of Chicago Press, 1966), pp. 77–83.

10. Bowen and Finegan, p. 387.

11. *Ibid*, p. 297. These figures are adjusted to control for the effect of factors other than schooling.

12. *Ibid*, p. 561, Table 1-C. Data for 1900–1950 are based on the work of Clarence Long. The data refer to the total labor force (including the armed forces) rather than the civilian labor force alone.

13. Mincer, pp. 78–80.

14. The example assumes for convenience that the unemployed, except for unemployed added workers, are distributed one to a household and that each household has at least one member outside the labor force who might be induced to enter it under certain circumstances. Dropping these assumptions would not affect the argument. Note that the original unemployed can drop out of the labor force, so that not all discouraged workers are potential new entrants.

15. Of course, this is not the same as a 1-percent rise in the rate. If the rate is 5 percent, a 1-point increase would be an increase of 20 percent.

Hours of Work and the Supply of Effort

VARIATION IN HOURS OF WORK

The amount of labor that workers supply obviously depends on the number of hours per week they are willing to work as well as on the number of people in the labor force in a given week. Unfortunately, the supply aspects of hours of work have been relatively neglected in the literature.

Before turning to the theory of hours of work, let us look at a few of the salient facts. First, it is clear that there has been a long-term decline in average hours, as shown in Table 4. At the turn of the century most industries had an average workweek of more than 50 hours, while now the average workweek is under 40 hours. It is much less clear what has been the role of supply forces, demand forces, and institutional changes in causing this decline in the workweek; we shall return to this subject later on.

The second important fact is that at any given time there is substantial variation in the hours worked by different members

19

TABLE 4

Average Hours of Work per Week in Manufacturing, Railroads, and Coal Mining, Selected Years, 1900–1957[a]

Year	Manufacturing	Railroads	Bituminous Coal
1900	55.0	52.3	42.8
1910	52.2	52.3	38.9
1920	48.1	48.0	39.3
1929	48.0	44.8	38.1
1939	37.3	42.1	26.8
1948	38.8	43.7	32.6
1957	37.8	36.5	31.5

[a] The concept of hours used is the annual aver·age of hours per week *actually worked* (not hours paid for) , so that an increase in paid leave time such as holidays and vacations results in a reduction of the average workweek as measured in these series. The years shown were selected so as to avoid recession years.

Source: Ethel B. Jones, "New Estimates of Hours of Work Per Week and Hourly Earnings, 1900–1957," *Review of Economics and Statistics* **45** (November 1963) , 375.

TABLE 5

Percentage Distribution of Hours of Work Per Week, July 1971

Hours of Work	Nonagricultural Industries	Agriculture
1–4	0.8	1.6
5–14	3.8	6.0
15–29	10.6	14.7
30–34	5.7	6.3
35–39	7.2	4.9
40	45.0	11.0
41–48	11.2	7.1
49–59	8.5	10.4
60 and over	7.2	38.0
Total at work	100.0	100.0

Source: U.S. Department of Labor, Bureau of Labor Statistics, *Employment and Earnings*, August 1971, Table A-22. The figures are obtained from household interviews in the Current Population Survey.

of the work force. Table 5 gives the percentage distributions of hours worked at all jobs for a week in July 1971. Although 45 percent of those at work outside agriculture reported working exactly 40 hours, the prevailing standard workweek, there were many people who worked much less or much more.

The common view is that employers establish hours and that workers must accept them if they are to have jobs. This demand-dominated view contains an important element of truth, but the reality is more complicated. Part-time work illustrates the importance of supply forces. Many women and students want to work only part time because of commitments at home or at school, and many succeed in finding regular part-time jobs. Of the 15 million people who worked part time (less than 35 hours a week) in the survey week of July 1971, almost 10 million usually worked part time and more than 5 million of these clearly did not want full-time jobs. Another 1.7 million preferred full-time jobs but could not find them.[1]

In some cases workers may take full-time jobs because they cannot find part-time jobs. In other cases employers create part-time jobs when they cannot find full-time employees; for example, they fill one full-time position with two half-time workers.

Just as there are people who want to work less than the standard workweek, there are others who want to work more. Those who want more income than they can get from a single job can hold two or more jobs at once. Many multiple jobholders, or *moonlighters*, are young married men with heavy family responsibilities and relatively low rates of pay. In May 1969, an estimated 4 million workers (5.2 percent of all employed) held two or more jobs at once. Only 658 thousand of these multiple jobholders were women. Almost half had worked on their secondary job the whole previous year. Especially high rates of multiple jobholding were reported for male teachers (17 percent) and for protective service workers—largely policemen, guards, and watchmen—whose rate was also 17 percent.[2] In Table 5 multiple jobholders are included among those working long total hours.

Having looked briefly at the variation, about the standard, of the actual workweek, we turn to the forces that influence the length of the standard week itself. These include market forces on the supply and demand sides as well as legislation and collective bargaining. We begin with the supply forces.

THE THEORY OF CHOICE
BETWEEN WORK AND LEISURE

The purpose of the formal theory of labor supply is to show how a rational decision maker would respond to changes in the opportunities facing him. This of course does not imply that all decisions about hours of work are rational, but if enough are, the theory will yield useful predictions.

The graphic presentation of the theory makes use of indifference maps, on which the indifference curves show constant levels of utility or satisfaction obtained from different combinations of work and leisure. For brevity the term *leisure* is used to indicate all activity except market work. Such an indifference map is shown in Figure 1, which assumes that the worker is free to choose

FIGURE 1
The Choice Between Hours of Work and Hours of Leisure

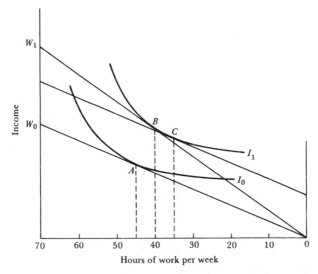

his hours at a constant wage per hour. The figure is drawn with income measured on the vertical axis and hours of work measured from right to left on the horizontal axis. This axis is arbitrarily cut off at the left at 70 hours per week.

The purpose of measuring the workweek "backwards" from right to left is to have the two axes of the diagram represent "goods" rather than "bads" when read in the usual way. The indifference curves then have their customary position, with increasing satisfaction shown by movement toward the northeast. The slope of the line from O to W_0 represents a constant hourly wage rate. The height of the line above any point on the horizontal axis measures the income earned by working that number of hours. The individual whose indifference map is shown would maximize his utility at A, where OW_0 is tangent to I_0, at 45 hours of work a week. If the wage rate then rises to OW_1, his new optimum is at B, where OW_1 is tangent to the higher indifference curve I_1. The number of hours supplied is reduced to 40. The individual's supply curve of hours in terms of wages cannot be read directly from Figure 1. It is obtained by plotting as points the slopes of opportunity lines such as OW_0, which represent wages rates, and plotting against them the corresponding number of hours supplied.

If opportunities for working more than some fixed number of hours are not open to the worker, this could be shown on the diagram by letting OW_0 become horizontal to the left of that number. The solution might then be located at the corner or kink in the opportunities line, since the horizontal portion would cross lower and lower indifference curves moving to the left, while the upward-sloping portion need not.

The diagram can also be used to show another kind of corner solution—the decision not to enter the labor force. This would occur if all the indifference curves were steeper than OW_0; the highest indifference curve would be reached at 0.

Following the Hicks method, we can use Figure 1 to decompose the change in hours caused by a wage increase into an income effect and a substitution effect. This is done by drawing the line parallel to OW_0 that is tangent to I_1 at C. The height of this line above OW_0 is the amount of nonlabor income that would be needed to make the worker as well off as he is after the wage increase without any change in the relative prices of labor and leisure. Since OW_1 is steeper than OW_0, which makes leisure more expensive in terms of earned income, C must lie to the right of B. As the figure is drawn, the wage increase reduces hours supplied from 45 to 40, while the equivalent increase in nonlabor income would reduce them to 35.

The horizontal distance from A to C, moving to the right, is the income effect of the wage change on hours of work. The horizontal distance from C to B, moving to the left, is the substitution effect. Their algebraic sum, the distance from A to B, is the total effect of the wage change on hours of work.

There is no necessary relation between the positions of either B or C and A. Placing C to the right of A involves the plausible assumption that leisure is a normal good (as distinguished from an inferior good), so that more of it is consumed when income rises and relative prices are unchanged. Placing B to the right of A involves the much stronger assumption that the income effect of the wage increase is larger than the substitution effect. Nothing in utility theory requires that the curves be placed so that this condition is satisfied. However, both the historical reduction in average hours of work and the evidence from cross-section analysis suggest that it has in fact been satisfied in most cases.[3]

THE OPTIMAL LENGTH OF THE WORKWEEK

Let us now try to use the apparatus described in the last section to see how the length of the workweek might be determined in a competitive economy. Under certain assumptions that are an oversimplification of reality, Figure 1 could completely explain this determination. These assumptions are:

a. that labor and product markets are competitive;
b. that all workers have the same unchanging set of preferences concerning the choice between income and leisure;
c. that there are no costs of employment other than hourly wages;[4] and
d. that the productivity of all workers in each hour is independent of the length of the workweek.

The last two of these assumptions taken together make employers indifferent to the number of hours worked per man; they would as soon have one man working 70 hours a week as two men working 35 hours each. Under these assumptions the demand for manhours cannot be decomposed into a demand for men and a demand for hours per man.

The first two assumptions assure that, given the competitively determined wage, an employer who selects a workweek other than the preferred one will be at a competitive disadvantage and will be unable to attract labor. He is selecting a position on OW_0 to the right or left of A, which for all workers lies on an indifference curve lower than I_0. If he attempts to offset his undesirable choice of hours by offering a higher hourly rate, his costs will rise and he will suffer losses, since he must still charge the competitive market price for his product. Under these conditions the history of hours of work, as real wages per hour rose through time, would trace out a series of points such as A and B, which are entirely determined by workers' preferences.

If we relax assumption (b), that all workers have the same preferences, then there will be dispersion in the workweeks set by different employers. Some employers will offer long workweeks to attract the workers with the strongest preferences for money income, while others will offer shorter workweeks to attract workers with the strongest preferences for leisure. If there is an oversupply of workers with a given set of preferences, employers who offer the corresponding number of hours will be able to hire labor at less than the prevailing wage (or to hire superior workers at that wage), and they will therefore have a competitive advantage. This will induce other employers to alter their workweeks so as to eliminate the excess supply or the below-normal wage at this number of hours. Hours of work, though no longer uniform, will still be entirely supply determined.

The fact that the labor force is not homogeneous in terms of age and sex is sufficient to insure that preferences for hours will not be uniform. Students, housewives, and the elderly can be expected to prefer shorter hours, either because of their commitments to nonmarket work or because they are physically less vigorous than prime-age males. If capital markets are imperfect, young husbands who are acquiring houses, cars, or household appliances will seek to work longer hours as an alternative to borrowing at high interest rates or to deferring consumption if they cannot borrow at all.

Additional interesting possibilities are opened up by relaxing assumption (d). At any particular place and time, there should be some function that relates output per hour to the number of hours worked per man. Up to some point this function might be linear, but eventually, as hours are increased, output per hour should decrease. As hours are increased still further, fatigue intensifies until the additional output becomes zero or negative. The optimal hours for a self-employed person could be determined by substituting the curve just described for the opportunities line OW_0 in Figure 1, whose slope is the wage rate. The new function might coincide with OW_0 at the right-hand side of the scale, but it would become flatter and eventually turn down as it moves left. The optimal combination of income and leisure would then be found where this productivity function was tangent to an indifference curve. (There can, of course, be only one such point if indifference curves are convex to the origin, since the output-hours function is concave.)

It is often alleged that in the early days of the industrial revolution employers chose a workweek so long that total weekly output per man could have been increased by shortening it.[5] If this had been true, any employer could have both increased the satisfaction of his workers and increased his output at no cost by working shorter hours and holding the weekly wage constant. He would then presumably have had a competitive advantage that would have forced other employers to follow him. Assuming collusion among employers is not sufficient to rationalize this view, since they would have been colluding against their own interests, whether viewed individually or collectively. The argument requires that all employers be either ignorant or shortsighted. For example, K. W. Rothschild argues that the beneficial effects of shorter hours on output are felt only after the passage of some time, and that no employer is willing to try the experiment of shortening hours for a long enough period to observe these effects.[6]

The possibility cannot be ruled out that at very low real wages, the optimum position of workers lies quite far to the left in terms of Figure 1, and that with habituation and a less intense pace of work, output could continue to rise with increases in the workweek well beyond any number of hours we would now regard as reasonable. Much of the empirical evidence usually cited to show the adverse effect of long hours on output comes from studies of abnormally long hours in wartime. These hours were worked by workers who either were acustomed to shorter hours or were new wartime recruits to the labor force, unaccustomed to industrial work. They worked long hours at high money wages at a time when there was a severe shortage of consumer goods. In these circumstances the number of hours that would maximize output may well have been in the neighborhood of 54 per week, with extensions beyond this offset by a slower work pace and more absenteeism and tardiness. This evidence is not inconsistent with an output-maximizing figure of 60 or even 72 hours a week a century earlier.

Below the point at which longer hours reduce output, abandoning the assumption of competition could clearly make it possible to frustrate the influence of worker preferences on hours of work. By custom or agreement employers could keep to a workweek that was too long (to the left of *A* in Figure 1) and confront most workers with the choice of working too much or not at all. In these circumstances, legislation or trade-union action would be needed to reduce the workweek. The possibility of impediments to the working of competition in reducing hours, at least in the short run, is increased by the lumpiness of some decisions to change hours, especially in continuous-process industries. For example, the American steel industry in 1923 moved in one jump from the 12-hour day to the 8-hour day by adding a third shift. Such a choice may mean moving initially from a workweek that is "too long" to one that is "too short," which helps to explain why steel lagged far behind other industries in shortening the workweek.

Up to this point our discussion of hours of work has been entirely in terms of the number of hours per week. In the years since World War II, however, reductions in the length of the work year have largely taken a different form, that of increases in paid vacations and holidays. These increases do not show up in the official statistics on the length of the workweek, which measures hours paid for and therefore treat an hour of paid leave as identical with an hour of work. The official statistics thus give the erroneous impression that the historical downward trend of hours ended in the 1930s.

There is good reason why, after the workweek has reached reasonable levels, further decreases in working time should take the form of more vacations and holidays rather than shorter hours in each workday. Vacations and holidays, especially holidays falling on Monday or Friday, create blocks of free time that can be used for trips or for substantial projects of work in the household. They reduce commuting time as well as working time, so that more time is saved for recreation or for household work than is lost at the job. With a 40-hour week, if the time involved in an extra week of paid vacation were spread across each of say 240 working days in a year it would amount to only 10 minutes a day, a change so slight that the worker would derive little benefit from it.

Very recently there have been some experiments with regular 4-day weeks, which may or may not involve a reduction in total hours. For example, a week of five 8-hour days could be changed to four 10-hour days. This not only cuts total commuting time but makes it possible for workers to commute at hours when there is less congestion on highways or transit systems. A number of firms report general satisfaction with such work patterns, including higher productivity and decreased absenteeism. It is too soon, however, to say whether a 4-day workweek will become common.

OVERTIME HOURS AND SHIFT WORK

So far we have been discussing cases in which all hours per week are paid at the same rate. However, it has now become almost universal practice to pay blue-collar workers for hours beyond the standard workweek at higher rates, which can be viewed as premium rates if the emphasis is on the supply response or as penalty rates if one focuses on the demand side. In the United States overtime is almost always paid at 1.5 times the straight-time rate; practice varies more in Britain, where 1.25 and 1.33 times the straight-time rate are often used.

Figure 2 shows the response to overtime premiums. Let us assume that if no overtime were paid, the worker would be in equilibrium at point D working 40 hours per week. If an overtime premium of time-and-a-half beyond 40 hours is introduced and overtime work is freely available, the new opportunities confronting the worker are shown by the broken line ODB. He would then choose the position E on indifference curve I_1, which is higher than the indifference curve (not shown) passing through the original position D. His hours of work now rise from 40 to 50. The straight-time wage that produces the same income as DB at 50 hours is OC, which also passes through E. But if the alternatives depicted by OC were open to the worker, he would choose not E but F, lying on the still higher indifference curve I_2. At F, hours

FIGURE 2
The Effect of Overtime Premiums

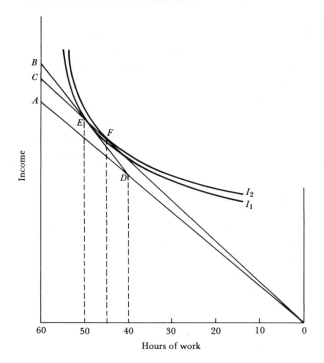

of work are shown in the diagram as higher than they were originally, though this need not always be true. But it will always be true that an increase in weekly income in the form of an overtime premium will call forth more hours of work than an equivalent increase in straight-time rates.

In fact, however, employers seldom offer overtime work in unlimited amounts. If there were no costs of hiring and training new workers and no fringe benefits, employers would always prefer to hire additional workers rather than to pay penalty rates. In the presence of hiring and training costs and fringe-benefit costs, the amount of planned overtime will depend on the relative importance of these costs and the overtime premium, as well as on worker preferences.

Where limited amounts of overtime are available at premium rates, workers are usually eager to get it, and opportunities to work overtime must be rationed by seniority. This suggests that over-time premiums are usualy larger than are needed to call forth the extra hours demanded. In other words, the effect of paying time-and-a-half beyond 40 hours is largely that of a penalty rate to discourage employers from using regular overtime schedules. Of course, the willingness of workers to work overtime at premium rates does not imply that standard hours are too short. To show this, one would need to show that workers wanted to work more hours at straight-time rates.

The motives of unions in bargaining for a shorter standard work-week or higher premium pay for overtime hours may differ from case to case. In a few cases the union may expect the same number of hours to be actually worked under a shorter standard work-week, so that the whole effect of the change is to increase weekly pay. In other cases, especially during recessions, the motive may be to spread work among a larger number of people and thus to reduce unemployment. This is also a frequent motive for legislated changes in the standard workweek.

The supply of hours depends not only on the length of the workweek but also on the pattern of hours during the week. As production becomes more capital intensive, there is a growing incentive for management to operate facilities with more than one shift. In continuous-processing operations, such as steel mills and petroleum refineries, it is necessary for the plant to operate 168 hours a week. Yet workers are in general reluctant to work night shifts or on weekends. Another undesirable working pattern is the split shift, often necessary in urban and suburban transporta-tion, in which a worker works 4 hours during the morning rush and another 4 hours during the evening rush.

The problem of undesirable working hours can be dealt with through the rotation of shifts or through payment of premium rates for undesirable shifts. In the United States these premiums (unlike overtime premiums) are generally set too low to overcome worker aversion to night and split shifts; thus in the absence of rotation these shifts are worked by the workers with least seniority or those at the greatest disadvantage in the labor market. It is not at all clear why unions have not made higher shift premiums a more important goal in bargaining, or why employers have re-sisted them.

THE SUPPLY
OF EFFORT

The theory of the supply of effort has been much less developed than the theory of hours of work. The pace of work should be faster where hours are short than where they are very long, since a worker cannot sustain an intense pace for long periods. There should also be an increase, within some range, in the intensity of work as real wages rise. Where real wages are very low, a wage increase may call forth a greater supply of effort simply because better paid workers will have a more adequate diet and better medical care and will therefore, for essentially biological reasons, be able to work harder.[7] This effect can no longer be of any appreciable importance in developed countries, where the wages of almost all fully employed workers will permit an adequate diet, if not necessarily an appealing one.

For developed countries the main effect of the level of wages on the supply of effort probably operates through the kind of supervision exercised by management. If labor is cheap, the costs of a leisurely work pace are not too great. If labor is expensive, the employer will take greater care to see that it is not wasted. However, the extent to which the pace of work can be controlled by supervision is limited by custom and by the protective role of the trade union. Attempts to force a pace of work that workers regard as unreasonable, even though it is one that has been achieved elsewhere, can lead to resistance of various forms, including failure to carry out the work properly. This is true in nonunion as well as unionized establishments.

The pace of work can be influenced also by the use of piecework or other incentive payment schemes. Where the pace of work is under the control of the individual worker, as in sewing garments or picking fruits and vegetables, individual piece rates are frequently used. Where cooperation among workers is important, various kinds of group incentives covering departments, establishments, or whole enterprises may be used.

Even where payment is strictly proportional to output (straight piecework), the employer gains from a faster pace of work, since costs other than direct labor costs (capital and indirect labor) are lower per unit of output when work is done faster. Trade unions seldom permit the use of straight piecework; in general they insist on some minimum guaranteed hourly rate and some payment for time when the worker is idle through no fault of his own, such as breakdowns of equipment or lack of supplies.

Piece rates or incentive pay may induce some workers with high needs for income or unusual stamina to want to work at a very rapid pace. In such cases the supply of effort is generally regulated by the work group in both union and nonunion situations.[8] This regulation arises from the desire to prevent less able workers from being shown up as inadequate or lazy, and to prevent the employer from making the achievements of a few into a standard for all. The control often takes the form of a quota of work or *bogey* which no one is to exceed; those who do may be ostracized or even threatened with physical harm. Workers who have completed their quota may appear to keep busy at work or may be permitted to play cards or take other forms of leisure on the job, such as long coffee breaks. If technical change makes a job easier, traditional work quotas can become unreasonably low. In such circumstances the employer often attempts to renegotiate the effort bargain by offering other advantages in return for a more reasonable work pace.

The presence of leisure on the job illustrates the difficulty of making a strict separation between working time and nonworking time. Those inclined to be indignant about the restriction of output by manual workers should remember that every occupational group has its own ways of combining work and leisure. The advertising executive who takes a client to a two-hour lunch may be working hard by the standards of his profession, but to a manual worker he would appear to be engaged solely in conspicuous consumption.

Group restrictions on the pace of work can also be present when payment is according to time worked and not directly related to output. In such cases the motive may be the fear of using up the available work too quickly and working oneself out of a job. Restrictive practices arising from this kind of fear should diminish under sustained full employment.

The relations between hours of work, the pace of work, and the level of real wages are complex. At any one time hours of work and the effort put forth by workers may seem to be governed by custom, law, and bargaining institutions. Over longer periods, however, they respond in reasonably predictable ways to changes in technology and in the level of real wages. Actual hours of work are gradually reduced as the level of living rises, while shorter hours and higher wages make possible and necessary a more sustained work effort during the time spent on the job.

NOTES

1. This paragraph is based on U.S. Department of Labor, Bureau of Labor Statistics, *Employment and Earnings*, August 1971, Table A-23.
2. See U.S. Department of Labor, Bureau of Labor Statistics, *Special Labor Force Report, Multiple Jobholders*, May 1969.
3. See in particular T. A. Finegan, "Hours of Work in the United States: A Cross Sectional Analysis," *Journal of Political Economy* **70** (October 1962), 452–470.
4. This assumption, though needed here, will not be discussed until Chapter 5, when the employer's choice between more hours and more men is considered.
5. For a good example of this view, see K. W. Rothschild, *The Theory of Wages*, 2d ed. (Oxford: Blackwell, 1965), pp. 50–55. The point of maximum output is sometimes called the point of optimum hours, which is a usage of the word "optimum" different from that in the text.
6. *Ibid*, p. 55.
7. The relation of this case to the demand for labor is considered in Chapter 5.
8. For a classic study of such restriction, see Stanley B. Mathewson, *Restriction of Output Among Unorganized Workers* (New York: Viking, 1931).

The Supply of Skill:
Investment in Human Capital

AN OVERVIEW

In addition to their mere presence at the workplace and willingness to work, almost all workers bring to their jobs some skill and experience. Skills are acquired either through schooling or through experience accompanied by formal or informal on-the-job training; both schooling and on-the-job training are forms of investment in human capital. Other forms of investment in human capital include expenditures to improve the workers' health and the costs of migration to a labor market where employment opportunities are better. The first of these will not be considered explicitly; treatment of the second is deferred to Chapter 6.

The analysis of investment in human capital is important for two kinds of reasons. First, it provides one of the main explanations for wage differentials by age and occupation. Second, with respect to policy, such analysis helps us consider how much of its resources an economy should devote to schooling and training relative to the resources it invests in such other areas as research and development or physical capital. The analysis also helps us consider who should pay for investment in schooling—the student himself and his parents, or society.

The importance of historical changes in skill level is suggested by the changes in occupational distribution shown in Table 6. Since 1900 there has been a sharp decline in the proportion of the work force who are farm workers or nonfarm laborers and a striking growth in the number of workers in white-collar occupations, especially professional and technical workers and clerical workers. The proportion of males who are skilled craftsmen has also grown.

A second way of looking at the growth of skills is illustrated in Table 7, which gives the median educational attainment of the labor force. These data are available on a consistent basis only for the years since 1952. The average member of the labor force in 1971, however, had completed one and a half more years of school than had his counterpart in 1952, and the gain for males was two years.

The proposition that a trained worker, like a machine, represents a valuable investment is a very old one in the history of economics. In both cases, making the investment requires a sacrifice of current consumption in order to increase future output. More precise analysis of the nature and role of human capital is quite recent; it owes much of its present development to the work of T. W. Schultz and Gary Becker.[1] The market for human capital differs from that for physical capital in that human capital is always rented rather than sold (except, historically, for slave economies). The market is for the services of the capital rather than for the capital stock or capital goods. This is the major reason why most of the investment in schooling is made by students or their families, and much of the rest is made by governments or such nonprofit institutions as foundations and universities. Commercial interests invest very little in human capital, although there has been a recent growth in bank loans to finance college education. It is sometimes asserted that the nontransferability of property rights in human capital (that is, the prohibition of slavery) inhibits the development of a commercial market for investment in people. This suggests that losses through default are expected to be higher on loans without collateral to finance college

TABLE 6

Percentage Distribution of Workers[a] by Major Occupation Group, 1900, 1950, and 1971

Males	1900	1950	1971
White-collar workers			
Professional and technical workers	3.4	7.2	13.7
Managers, proprietors, and officials	6.8	10.5	14.6
Clerical workers	2.8	6.4	6.7
Sales workers	4.6	6.4	5.9
Blue-collar workers			
Craftsmen and foremen	12.6	19.0	19.9
Operatives	10.3	20.6	18.3
Nonfarm laborers	14.7	8.8	7.7
Service workers			
Private household workers	0.2	0.2	0.1
Other service workers	2.9	6.0	8.1
Farm workers			
Farmers and farm managers	23.0	10.0	3.2
Farm laborers and foremen	18.7	4.9	1.9
Total	100.0	100.0	100.1

Females	1900	1950	1971
White-collar workers			
Professional and technical workers	8.2	12.2	14.5
Managers, proprietors, and officials	1.4	4.3	5.0
Clerical workers	4.0	27.4	33.9
Sales workers	4.3	8.6	7.2
Blue-collar workers			
Craftsmen and foremen	1.4	1.5	1.3
Operatives	23.7	20.0	13.3
Nonfarm laborers	2.6	0.9	0.8
Service workers			
Private household workers	28.7	8.9	4.9
Other service workers	6.7	12.6	17.4
Farm workers			
Farmers and farm managers	5.9	0.7	0.3
Farm laborers and foremen	13.1	2.9	1.4
Total	100.0	100.0	100.0

[a] The base of these percentages differs for each year shown. In 1900 it is all gainful workers (those having a usual occupation); in 1950 it is the labor force 14 years of age and older, which includes the employed and the unemployed; in 1971 it is employed workers 16 years of age and older. These changes in the base are not large enough to affect the major trends appreciably.

Source: Gertrude Bancroft, *The American Labor Force: Its Growth and Changing Composition*, New York: Wiley, 1958, Table D-2; and *Manpower Report of the President*, March 1972, Table A-11.

TABLE 7

Median Years of School Completed by the Civilian Labor Force,
18 Years Old and Over, Selected Dates

	Both Sexes	Male	Female
October 1952	10.9	10.4	12.0
March 1962	12.1	12.0	12.2
March 1971	12.4	12.4	12.5

Source: *Manpower Report of the President,* March 1972, Table B-9.

education than on loans with physical or financial collateral, although there does not appear to be any evidence that they actually are. No equities market for investment in people has developed, though efforts are being made to devise one. Such investment would take the form of loans to students, which would be repaid, not in the form of principal plus stated interest, but as some fraction of the students' earnings after graduation.[2]

Skills acquired by schooling beyond the legally required minimum are supplied by people who voluntarily take additional schooling at a cost to themselves in return for higher money or psychic incomes later. The supply of skills can therefore be increased by lowering the private costs of schooling, by increasing the earnings of workers who have completed more years of schooling, or by other improvements in the prestige or satisfactions of skilled work.

THE PRIVATE RATE
OF RETURN ON SCHOOLING

In order to study the effect of investment on earnings we make use of age-earnings profiles, which show the average annual earnings, in a given year, of people of different ages who have had the same amount of schooling. Such profiles typically show that earnings rise early in life as workers gain in experience and maturity; reach a peak in middle life; and then decline as the waning of health, strength, and quickness of mind becomes a more important force than further accumulation of experience.[3] Note that we are not suggesting that the earnings of a given cohort of individuals decline after middle age, but only that they then earn less than the next younger cohort.

Three age-incomes profiles, for different levels of schooling, are shown in Table 8. Median income is lower for all three educational levels after the age of 54. The low median incomes of the youngest college graduates presumably reflect the fact that many did not work the whole of the previous year. It would be more relevant to show *earnings* by age and educational attainment rather than *income*, which includes income from property. But comparable data for earnings by such detailed age categories are not available.

The process of investment in schooling is illustrated for the case of college education in Figure 3. Money earnings and the out-of-pocket costs of education to the individual (tuition, books, and so on) are measured on the vertical axis; age is measured on the horizontal axis. (For clarity, the scale for the college years, 18–22, is twice as large as it should be relative to the length of working life after college.) Curves *A* and *B* are the earnings profiles of two individuals . Mr. *B* enters the labor market at age 18 on graduation from high school and works until retirement at age 65. Mr. *A* attends college, incurring out-of-pocket costs for four years. These

TABLE 8

Selected Data on Median Income of Males with Income by Age and Educational Attainment, 1959

Age in 1960	Years of School Completed		
	Elementary 8	High School 4	College 4
16 and 17	$ 630	$ 750	—
18 and 19	1155	1057	—
20 and 21	1914	2442	$1751
22–24	2712	3496	2852
25–29	3683	4745	5477
30–34	4293	5452	7365
35–44	4541	5848	8669
45–54	4609	5806	8949
55–64	4278	5413	8345
65–74	2095	2969	5236
75 and over	1312	1727	3017

Source: U.S. Census of Population, 1960, *Subject Reports.* Educational Attainment, Table 6.

FIGURE 3
Investment in Schooling

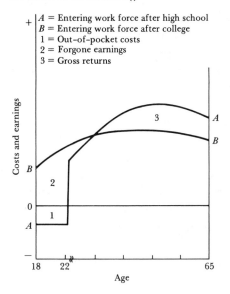

A = Entering work force after high school
B = Entering work force after college
1 = Out-of-pocket costs
2 = Forgone earnings
3 = Gross returns

costs are shown by the position of the left end of his curve, which lies below zero on the vertical axis. In addition he forgoes the earnings made by *B*, which he, too, could have earned if he had entered the labor force at 18. The sum of the forgone earnings and the out-of-pocket costs is his investment in college education. In practice, earnings from jobs during vacations and part-time jobs during the school year may offset much of the out-of-pocket costs. Note that the cost of subsistence while in school is not included. To count both subsistence and forgone earnings would be double counting, since Mr. *B* also has costs of subsistence, which he pays out of his earnings.

In general, forgone earnings represent a much larger part of the private costs of education (those incurred by the student and his family) than do out-of-pocket costs. This suggests that the provision of free tuition and books would have only a small effect in reducing income differentials caused by differences in educational attainment. In order to achieve a larger effect it would be necessary to provide stipends or grants to college students to replace forgone earnings and simultaneously to provide a large number of places for students. The effect of thus enlarging the supply of those with college training would be to lower the earnings differential they command.

As Figure 3 is drawn, A's earnings when he enters the labor market do not immediately equal B's, since B has meanwhile been receiving on-the-job training. The forgone earnings associated with attending college thus extend beyond the actual period of attendance. This is not a necessary feature of the diagram; it could have been drawn so that A's earnings were greater than, or equal to, B's earnings from the time he went to work.

At some time after A enters the labor force, his earnings surpass B's and remain higher for the rest of his working life. The area lying below A's profile and above B's, to the right of the point where they cross, is the gross return on college education. It might be more realistic to assume also that the person with more education will retire later (see Chapter 1). However, the added earnings would come at the end of working life and would be so heavily discounted as to have little effect on the present value of education at age 18.

There are two principal methods of deciding from profiles like those in Figure 3 whether investment in college education is economically productive. If A can borrow to finance his education at a known interest rate, both the costs and gross returns can be discounted back to age 18 at this interest rate to calculate the present value of the investment at that age. In choosing between two investment programs, an individual who seeks to maximize the economic return on his investment will choose the program with the highest present value. An investment program might consist of entering the labor market after graduating from high school or of completing four years of college instead. The present-value formula in this case is:

$$V = \sum_{i\,=\,18}^{65} \frac{Y_i}{(1 + r)^{i-18}}$$

where V is the present value at age 18, r is the rate of interest, Y is earnings or cost in a particular year (negative values indicating costs), and i designates age. The present value of either program will of course be smaller, the higher the interest rate. Indeed, V can be negative at high interest rates even if total costs are smaller than gross returns, because the costs are all incurred before the returns begin.

The alternative method of calculation is to find a reasonable rate of interest at which the present value of the investment is zero because the costs and returns are exactly equal when discounted back to age 18 at this rate. Such a rate is known as an internal rate of return. However, the typical investment in schooling may have more than one internal rate of return because the returns cover a number of periods.

The relation between present values and internal rates of return is shown in Figure 4, in which X and Y are two investment programs. The intercept of the curves on the vertical axis is simply the excess of undiscounted returns over undiscounted costs, since the interest rate at the vertical axis is zero. The points at which each of the curves crosses the line indicating zero present value give two internal rates of return, r_x and r_y. The example has been chosen to illustrate the possibility that the curves can cross because of differing time patterns of costs and returns. Investment program X, with higher undiscounted net returns, has a lower internal rate of return because more of the benefits lie in the distant future. For purposes of social or educational planning, if the internal

FIGURE 4
Present Values of Two Investments

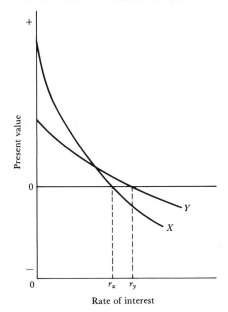

rates of return on two competing programs of investment in human capital lie much above prevailing rates of return on physical capital (which is entirely possible, given the imperfections of the market for human capital), one should not conclude that more investment should be made in the program with the higher internal rate. It is more relevant to rank the programs according to their present values calculated at interest rates in the neighborhood of prevailing returns on equally risky investments in physical capital.

Calculations of the rate of return on schooling often show higher returns for the years in which stages of education are completed than for intermediate years. Thus the return on the fourth year of college exceeds that on the previous three. It seems unlikely that the amount of investment through education is actually higher in the fourth year; it would be more logical to expect diminishing returns to successive years in a program. The bonus for completion of a program is more likely to reflect personal attributes that are valued by employers and that are more likely to be present among graduates than among dropouts—such as the determination needed to finish tasks undertaken.

It is not necessary for investment in schooling to take place before one begins a career; some people go back to school toward the middle of their working lives. However, investments in human capital made late in life, whether in schooling or in migration, tend to have lower rates of return than investments made in youth, because there is less time left in which they can yield benefits. Nevertheless, rapid technological progress in any field can make original investments in schooling obsolete and force skilled workers to learn new techniques. While this can often be done by reading or by learning on the job, it seems probable that going back to school in middle age will become more common than it has been. For example, doctors might return to medical school after 20 years of practice for intensive courses in new developments in medicine.

The foregoing account has dealt largely with private decisions made by students or their families to invest in schooling. For this purpose the returns should be measured net of taxes on earnings. Since income taxes are computed on progressive schedules based on annual earnings, they discriminate against people who undertake a long period of investment and then have higher annual earnings for a shorter working life. Such people pay more income taxes during their lifetime than people with identical net lifetime earnings who start work earlier.

SOCIAL RETURNS
ON EDUCATION

The analysis of the last section can easily be modified to deal with social or government decisions on investment in education. For this purpose the returns are calculated before deducting income and payroll taxes, and the costs include expenditures on education by governments and nonprofit institutions as well as expenditures by students and their families.

It is often objected that the kind of calculation we have been discussing errs in assuming that the value of education lies entirely in raising earnings, and the objection is well taken. It is obvious that education also has direct value as a consumer good, both while it is in progress and through enriching life after it is completed. Moreover, in making social decisions it should be taken into account that education may produce better informed and more responsible citizens, as well as simply producing better workers. Such arguments suggest that the return on education calculated from earnings is a minimum return—the lower bound of a true overall return. This implies that educational programs whose calculated return is very high schould be continued, and that even those whose calculated return is very low should not necessarily be discontinued. An extreme case is offered by a few long programs of training for occupations with low earnings, such as the ministry. For training in theology, calculated present values based on monetary rewards are substantially negative, but substantial nonpecuniary rewards are clearly involved for the individuals who pursue careers in religion, and perhaps for society as well.[4]

Other critics of the calculation of the social return on education from subsequent earnings argue that not all of the higher earnings of educated people represent their higher productivity. To some extent a diploma, especially one from a school or college with high prestige, is simply a way to get a preferred place in the queue for scarce, highly paid jobs. It is argued that the successful applicants are selected by previous graduates of the same schools or similar ones on the basis of loyalty and friendship rather than on the basis of potential performance. The duties of the men selected may then be relatively undemanding, while the difficult work gets done by those with less schooling or by graduates of schools with less prestige.

To the extent that this account of the operation of the "old boy network" is correct, the private return on education is higher than the social return, and education is merely a selection process rather than an investment process. Although there is an element of truth in this account, it is probably small and diminishing in the United States. Degrees clearly facilitate entry to good jobs, but criteria for promotion are increasingly based on performance rather than merely on social class and acceptable conduct; and college graduates who cannot perform may find themselves blocked from advancement. The increasing rationality of selection in a highly technical economy in turn promotes reference to practical rather than traditional values in shaping educational curricula.

SOME PROBLEMS
IN THE MEASUREMENT OF RETURNS

The data on which training decisions must be based show the earnings from various kinds of work of people engaged in it at a particular time. Such earnings profiles from cross-sectional data are not the same as the pattern of earnings traced through time by a cohort of people with the same training. The time profile will be raised by the growth of productivity, which counteracts the tendency of cross-sectional profiles to turn downward toward the end of working life, and moves the earnings peak to the right. The productivity effect is in part offset by allowing for the possibility of mortality or total disablement during the working life, which reduces the return to training. This, too, is not reflected in cross-sectional age-earnings profiles. Some researchers have made explicit allowance for productivity and mortality, though it is hard to find a firm basis for projecting trends in productivity into the future.

The analysis of returns to investment in schooling can be carried out for any kind of schooling for which both age-earnings profiles and cost data can be gathered. There is some question, however, about the validity of calculating private returns to schooling for years of schooling below normal school-leaving age. Children below this age are seldom employed except in family farms or businesses, so, in general, the earnings forgone by staying in school are small or zero. Most primary and secondary schools do not charge tuition, so out-of-pocket expenses are also very small. Furthermore, the need to supervise small children when they are not in school means that the private costs of primary schooling can be negative, especially to working mothers.

When differences in returns are related to a very small cost base, the rate of return will appear to be extremely high, but it will also be very sensitive to small changes in the cost estimates. What is being estimated is more the effect of compulsory schooling legislation and child labor laws than the productivity of investment in younger children. Such legislation requires people to invest more in training their children than they might choose to if unconstrained.

A more general and important problem in interpreting returns on training is the presence of correlation between amount of education and native ability. If the most able people also get the most education, some part of the estimated return to education is in fact a return to ability. Since the correlation is far from perfect, it is possible in principle to correct the estimates to allow for it. Some corrections of this kind have been made in several studies. For example, Becker finds that adjusting rates of return by measures of ability causes only a very slight reduction in the estimated rates of return.[5] The available data are far from perfect, however, and better data might modify this conclusion.

OCCUPATIONAL TRAINING

It is useful at this point to distinguish between a skill and an occupation. A skill may be defined as the ability to perform a particular task well. An occupation is a line of work whose practitioners use a particular combination of skills, or one of a related set of combinations, to contribute to the production of some marketable good or service. Some skills, when not pursued entirely as a hobby, are useful in only one occupation and are the principal requirement for following that occupation (for example, cutting hair or flying an airplane). Others are useful in a wide variety of occupations, though they may be the principal requirements for some (for example, writing good prose). Students who have not yet developed a strong preference for a particular occupation or who are uncertain about their prospects in various occupations can hedge by investing in skills with multiple uses.

Since we cannot directly observe the incomes produced by having particular skills, we must use data on income by occupation to measure the returns to choices of kinds of skill (as distinguished from length of schooling). The earnings profiles of Figure 3 can be modified for this purpose so that each profile represents an occupation. The periods of training could coincide in whole or in part but could differ in cost because of differences in tuition rates or in the availability of scholarships or fellowships. Young people trying to decide which of the two occupations to enter would tend to choose the one where the present value of the income stream is higher. Such comparisons are not intended to suggest that these calculations are made explicitly or that they dominate decisions on occupational choice or the kind of training to undertake. Personal tastes and interests and the influence of parents, teachers, and friends play major and often controlling roles. Yet for many students, tastes and advice are not decisive; for these the influence of economic rewards is probably important.

Because many skills have multiple uses, it is possible for those who are trained for one occupation to end up working in another. Corporation executives are often trained in law, engineering, or accounting rather than in management, and they are in general better paid than their former colleagues who still work at their original professions. The observations on the earnings of these executives will not appear in statistics on the earnings of those who continued working as lawyers, engineers, or accountants, and their absence will bias downward the estimates of rates of return to training in these professions.

The age–earnings profile for an occupation shows only the mean earnings of its practitioners and not the dispersion of earnings. But dispersion also influences occupational choices. Adam Smith argued that where many of those who train for a profession will not succeed in it, the returns to those who do succeed should balance the costs of those who fail. He also felt that the presence of a few conspicuously high rewards in a profession, like high prizes in a lottery, would attract a number of entrants out of proportion to the true expectation of success.[6] But if some students are risk takers in their choice of careers, others are risk averters; these latter may be attracted to a career like teaching, despite the absence of large prizes, for the security it offers.[7]

The same kind of analysis used for occupations where training takes place in schools or colleges can be extended to other kinds of training, such as apprenticeship. At one time apprenticeship often involved the payment of money by a boy's family to a master craftsman in return for the training the craftsman would provide. Less explicit costs are involved where an apprentice works for less than the wage he could have earned in an alternative occupation. Over the years, as training for the crafts has shifted in part from training by employers and journeymen to training in secondary schools, periods of formal apprenticeship have tended to begin later and become shorter, and wages of apprentices may even exceed those of operatives of the same age. In such cases, apprenticeship for a well-paid craft may have little or no economic cost to the apprentice, and large returns. Therefore access to apprenticeship programs has to be rationed—for example, by admitting only the sons and nephews of journeymen.

A union of craftsmen that wanted to restrict the supply of skills in order to avoid lowering the wages of the craft could do so in any of four ways. First, it could keep the wages of apprentices very low, thus raising the costs of training to the apprentice. Second, it could unduly prolong the period of apprenticeship, which would also raise the costs to the apprentice. Third, it could set the wages of apprentices very high, so that employers would not want to undertake the costs of training apprentices. Finally, it could simply limit the number of apprentices employers were permitted to train.[8]

Apprenticeship programs in which trade unions participate are not the major source of training of new entrants to most craft occupations. Less formal on-the-job training or employer-controlled apprenticeships in the nonunion sector provide a substantial portion of the supply of craft skills. The craft unions later admit as members some of the men so trained. Those not admitted can be prevented, by understandings between unions and unionized employers, from working in the union sector, but they can practice their craft at lower wages in the nonunion sector. However, the less formal kinds of training sometimes produce workers with a narrower range of skills than those of union journeymen.

On-the-job training offered by employers varies from formal programs not unlike those conducted by educational institutions to the simplest forms of learning by doing, observing others, and being reprimanded for mistakes. Since there are substantial economies of scale in conducting formal training programs, they tend to be run mainly by larger employers. The existence of returns to on-the-job training is indicated by the positive relation of earnings to both seniority and previous work experience, though the relation of earnings to seniority. may also have other sources, such as the need to maintain morale or conform to widely held concepts of equity.[9]

Training within a firm is undertaken at a cost. Where the training is clearly separable activity, these costs can be identified quite precisely. For example, training an airline pilot to fly a new type of aircraft involves costs that include the pay of the instructor and the trainee, the operating costs and capital costs of the aircraft used for training, and perhaps the cost of special materials or equipment used in training, such as flight simulators. Where training takes place concurrently with production, the costs, though of the same general kind, may be more difficult to measure. Some of the trainee's time and some of that of his supervisors or fellow workers is used in training; output is therefore less than it would be if all workers were fully trained. For the same reason, capital costs per unit of output may be higher than normal. Materials may be wasted in scrap or defective products owing to the trainee's inexperience. To minimize such costs, firms will usually prefer to rehire old employees or hire those who have had similar experience elsewhere in preference to hiring inexperienced workers. Employers also try to adopt personnel policies that encourage experienced workers to remain with the firm.

Gary Becker has introduced the very useful distinction between general training and specific training.[10] General training develops skills of equal value both in the organization that gives the training and elsewhere. In the literature on economic development, it is this general kind of training that is referred to in discussions of the problems of getting a rural population accustomed to the discipline of industrial work. Specific training is training in skills that are of greatest value to the employer who gives the training, either because he is a monopolist or because he has his own special methods, routines, and equipment with which newcomers must become familiar. In the case of specific training, pay during the training period will exceed the employee's net marginal product where this is defined as the trainee's contribution to value added, minus the costs of training. Especially for formal training, the net marginal product during the training period can be zero or negative.

The excess of wages over marginal product (which can be larger than the wage if the marginal product is negative) is the employer's investment in training. This investment can be recouped with interest over the period of the worker's employment with the firm by paying him slightly less than his marginal product after he is trained. The employee cannot earn more elsewhere, since his training is not of equal use to other employers. For any given rate of recoupment of costs per time period, the return on investment in specific training will depend on the length of employment. An unexpectedly high rate of turnover may produce losses on investment in specific training, while an unexpectedly low one would produce windfall gains.

For general training, there can be no appreciable wedge between marginal product and wages after the training period, since in a competitive labor market the employee could get wages equal to the full value of his marginal product from another employer. There will therefore be a tendency for the wages of trainees receiving general training to be kept down to the level of their net marginal product during the training period; thus the employee in effect pays for his own training through reduced wages while he is being trained.

General and specific training are perhaps best regarded as the ends of a continuum rather than as discrete alternatives. Much training contains elements of both, and some is specific to a small group of employers rather than to one. In the latter case, if there are economies of scale in training, the employers could undertake some cooperative training venture. At times it may pay one employer to offer training on generous terms even though some of those who complete the training will leave his employ. For example, in an industry of three firms, one of which produces half the total output, it might pay the largest firm to do all the training for some industry-specific occupation without forcing the trainees to bear the costs. It could expect to lose about half its trainees through turnover but might nevertheless get the highest possible return from this policy, which would attract able trainees and permit the firm to try to keep for itself the trainees who seemed to have the greatest ability.

THE SUPPLY CURVE OF LABOR: A SUMMARY

We can conclude and summarize our discussion of the supply of labor with a few remarks about supply schedules. A supply curve of man-hours to the economy as a whole, in which real hourly wages are plotted on the vertical axis and number of man-hours supplied is plotted on the horizontal axis, will probably be backward sloping at the average real wage levels of developed countries; that is, it will slope downward from left to right, unlike the usual supply curve. The backward slope arises from the tendency for hours of work per year to be reduced as real income rises, while the overall rate of labor-force participation for all groups in the population taken together remains roughly constant.

The supply curve of labor to any particular occupation, industry, or area must necessarily be forward sloping when measured against the wage for this employment relative to wages elsewhere. This will be true whether the supply is measured in number of men or in number of man-hours. Such curves slope forward because the higher relative wage attracts labor into this activity at the expense of others. The supply of labor to unskilled occupations is determined in part by the mobility of mature workers, and the supply curve could be quite flat even in the short run. For occupations using specialized skills requiring a long period of training, the short-run supply curve might be almost vertical. A pronounced forward slope would emerge only after a change in relative wages had produced a response through changes in the number undertaking training. However, such a long-run response would be absent only if the number of training places were somehow rigidly fixed or if decisions on career choice were based entirely on nonmonetary factors; neither of these conditions is likely to be met. Another improbable requirement also must be met for the long-run supply of labor to a patricular use to be completely inelastic: The rate of retirement and of transfer out of this employment in midcareer would have to be completely unaffected by the relative wage.

At the same time, there is good reason to believe that the supply of labor to an occupation will not usually be perfectly elastic even in the very long run.[11] The long-run supply would be perfectly elastic if occupations differed only in the cost of the training needed to enter them. Each occupation would then be able to attract an unlimited number of entrants by offering average annual earnings that exceeded the average earnings of an occupation requiring no training by a margin that, when discounted at the prevailing rate of interest, fully covered private training costs. Occupations differ, however, not only in the amount of training they require but also in the extent to which they call upon scarce innate talents and in the nonpecuniary advantages and disadvantages of working in them. These advantages and disadvantages will be evaluated differently by different people, which is sufficient to give the long-run supply curve an upward slope. To the extent that the disadvantages lie in the difficulty of doing work, they will see seem least important to those who have the relevant innate talents. As an occupation continues to expand, it must eventually recruit

FIGURE 5
The Short-Run and Long-Run Supply
of Labor to an Occupation

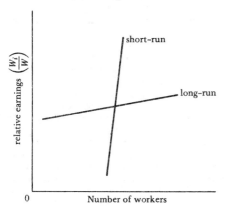

more people who do not find it congenial and who will therefore demand a higher return for entering it.[12]

The long-run and short-run supply curves of labor to an occupation requiring training are shown in Figure 5. The vertical axis measures annual earnings in this occupation relative to average annual earnings in all other occupations. The point of intersection of the two curves is the initial position at the time from which the long and short runs are reckoned. The short run may be defined as a period too short to train new entrants, so that the short-run curve is not vertical only because of the entry or exit from the occupation of those already trained. In general, the shapes of the curves reflect the arguments of the two preceding paragraphs, leading to the conclusion that short-run supply curves are not perfectly inelastic and long-run supply curves are not perfectly elastic.

NOTES

1. See especially T. W. Schultz, "Investment in Human Capital," *American Economic Review* (March 1961), 1–17; and Gary S. Becker, *Human Capital: A Theoretical and Empirical Analysis, with Special Reference to Education* (New York: National Bureau of Economic Research, 1964).
2. See K. Shell et al., "The Education Opportunity Bank: An Economic Analysis," *National Tax Journal* (March 1968), 2–45.
3. For an interesting summary of some psychological studies showing changes in selected mental abilities with age, see Harold Lydall, *The Structure of Earnings* (Oxford: Clarendon, 1968), pp. 113–117. These studies show a decline in nonverbal problem-solving ability after age 25 and in performance on a vocabulary test after middle age, except for the most able group.
4. See David A. A. Stager, "Monetary Returns to Post-Secondary Education in Ontario," unpublished doctoral dissertation, Princeton University, 1968.
5. Becker, pp. 79–88.
6. Adam Smith, *The Wealth of Nations*, bk. 1, chap. 10 (New York: Random House, 1937).
7. Consideration of risk may lead to an economic decision rule on how much or what kind of investment to make in education other than the rule of maximizing expected net earnings—for example, minimizing the probability that earnings will fall below some target figure. For an interesting analysis along these lines, see Stephan Michelson, "Rational Income Decisions of Negroes and Everybody Else," *Industrial and Labor Relations Review* 23 (October 1969), 15–28.
8. Professional associations not usually considered trade unions may play a similar role in limiting the number of places for students or trainees, as the American Medical Association did in the 1930s. See Milton Friedman and Simon Kuznets, *Income from Independent Professional Practice* (New York: National Bureau of Economic Research, 1945). Such policies will almost always be depicted as attempts to preserve reasonable standards of competence in the craft or profession and may be hard to distinguish from legitimate concern with standards. Organizational efforts to restrict entry to occupations can be reinforced by legislation requiring occupational licensing; such legislation raises

the same problem of distinguishing reasonable standards from unreasonable barriers.

9. For statistical evidence on the relation of seniority and experience to earnings, see A. Rees and G. P. Shultz, *Workers and Wages in an Urban Labor Market* (Chicago: University of Chicago Press, 1970), pp. 152–156.

10. Becker, pp. 8–28.

11. For a contrary view, see Belton M. Fleisher, *Labor Economics: Theory and Evidence* (Englewood Cliffs, N.J.: Prentice-Hall, 1970), p. 112.

12. The supply of labor to an occupation is discussed further in Chapter 11.

PART II

The Demand for Labor

CHAPTER 4

Marginal Productivity Theory in Competitive Markets

THE NATURE AND USES OF A THEORY OF THE DEMAND FOR LABOR

The basic purpose of a theory of the demand for labor is to determine how much labor employers will want to employ at different wage rates. Answers to this question are important in a variety of policy contexts. For example, if one raises the minimum wage, will many fewer low-wage workers be employed, or about the same number as before? If a union wins a wage increase in collective bargaining, will its members therefore have fewer hours of work than they had previously? Many similar examples can easily be imagined.

Where wages are determined in the market rather than by law or by collective bargaining, the theory of demand for labor has an important additional purpose—it becomes a major component of a theory of wage determination. To some extent, though less directly, it is also a component of the theory of wage determination under collective bargaining. However, as we shall see in a moment, a theory of demand can never comprise the whole of a theory of wage determination under any set of institutions.

In some cases labor is demanded for itself—as in hiring a babysitter. The demand for labor in such cases is identical with the demand for the service itself. In most cases, however, a particular kind of labor is used in combination with many other factors of production to produce a complex product or service, such as an automobile or a television broadcast. The demand for labor in this case is a derived demand, derived from the demand for the final product or service.

The generally accepted theory of the demand for labor has changed very little since the beginning of this century. It is an application of the *marginal productivity theory* of the demand for any factor of production in processes where two or more factors cooperate.[1] Although the theory has been severely attacked by institutional labor economists, it survives the attacks both because the critics have often misunderstood it and because they have conspicuously failed to develop a coherent alternative theory to put in its place.

Much of the misunderstanding of marginal productivity theory is summed up in the single unfortunate term "the marginal productivity theory *of wages*," a term that will be studiously avoided here for reasons made explicit long ago by Alfred Marshall.[2] A demand schedule is a functional relation between a price (in this case, a wage) and the quantity demanded. This relation does not uniquely determine the wage except in the highly unusual cases in which supply is perfectly inelastic. The demand schedule has no effect whatever on the wage in the cases at the other extreme of possible supply conditions, in which the supply curve confronting an employer is perfectly elastic. These cases include both the decisions of the individual firm under perfect competition and circumstances in which an employer is required by legislation or by trade-union action to pay a wage higher than he otherwise would. In these cases the demand schedule based on marginal productivity determines only the amount of labor employed. In all intermediate cases, wages and employment are jointly determined by supply and demand—the two "blades" of Marshall's metaphorical scissors. To speak of "the marginal productivity theory of wages" is exactly analogous to speaking of "the demand theory of prices," a term so ridiculous on its face that it is seldom used.

The discussion of this chapter will retain two simplifying assumptions introduced in Chapter 2: first, that there are no costs of employment other than hourly wages; and second, that the productivity of labor is independent of the length of the workweek. These assumptions permit the quantity of labor demanded to be expressed in man-hours without being decomposed into the number of hours and the number of men. Thus we again assume that the employer is indifferent toward one man working 70 hours per week or two men each working 35, provided that in both cases the capital equipment is working 70 hours. Variations in the length of time per week that the capital is working (say by adding a second or third shift) are ways of altering the ratio of inputs not ordinarily considered in formal discussions of marginal productivity theory. One would imagine that the diminishing returns to adding labor apply to each shift separately, and that if the productivity of the whole second shift is lower than that of the first, this has to be explained by the nature of the labor supply and the tastes of the workers.

The basic theory of the demand for labor in competitive markets is considered in this chapter. Chapter 5 considers departures from competition and some other extensions. Among these, we introduce the fixed costs of employment and discuss the separate demands for hours and for men.

THE DERIVATION
OF THE DEMAND SCHEDULE

Figure 6 illustrates the derivation of the short-run and long-run demand schedules for labor from a production function in which an output is produced by two inputs. The function represents for an unchanging technology all possible combinations of factor inputs, not all of which are necessarily in use anywhere. Man-hours of homogeneous labor per period of time are measured on the horizontal axis; units of capital services (machine-hours, if one likes), on the vertical axis. The main reason for measuring capital inputs as a flow of services rather than as a stock is to allow for differences in the life of capital equipment. A machine costing $10,000 and lasting 5 years is furnishing services that cost $2,000

FIGURE 6
A Production Function of Two Factors

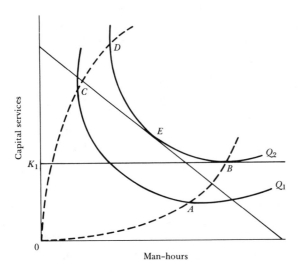

a year through depreciation, in addition to the cost of actual or imputed interest on its value. A machine of the same cost that lasted 10 years would be furnishing services corresponding to depreciation at only half this rate. The first machine would have to save more in labor or materials inputs in order to justify its use.

Output per period of time is measured in Figure 6 perpendicularly above the plane defined by the axes. The curved lines convex to the origin labeled Q_1 and Q_2 are *isoquants*, or loci of points at which output is equal. Thus at all points on Q_2 output is greater than at all points on Q_1. The amount of output represented by each can be specified, so the resulting diagram of the production surface is more analogous to a relief map in cartography than to an indifference map representing ordinal utility. These isoquants can be drawn as densely as one likes, but they cannot cross, since one point cannot denote two different outputs. Their convexity to the origin represents a diminishing marginal rate of substitution in production—the higher the proportion of one factor in the input mix, the more of it one would have to add to make up for the loss of one unit of the other factor. The short-run marginal product schedule of labor is derived by moving horizontally across the production surface above a line such as the one that intersects the vertical axis at K_1; such a line represents some fixed level of capital inputs. The height of the production surface above this line initially increases, as we move to the right, and measures changes in the total product as the quantity of labor is increased. The slope of this total product curve is the short-run marginal product schedule of labor, shown in Figure 7. In other words, the height of the marginal product schedule shows the addition to output obtained by using an additional man-hour of labor input, with inputs of capital services constant.

Point *B* in Figure 6, at which the line from K_1 is tangent to an isoquant, is the point at which total product is at a maximum for the given capital input; at this point the marginal product of labor is zero. Beyond this, so much labor is being used relative to the fixed amount of capital services that output could actually be increased by reducing labor inputs. There are so many workers that they are getting in one another's way or do not have the tools to do any useful work. An entrepreneur who maximizes short-run profits would operate at point *B* only if labor were free, and would never knowingly operate to the right of it. The locus of points such as *A* and *B* that are the lowest points of isoquants is shown by a dotted line in Figure 6. This is sometimes called a *ridge line*, because as one moves horizontally to the right it marks the point at which the production surface begins to slope downward.

FIGURE 7
A Marginal Productivity Schedule

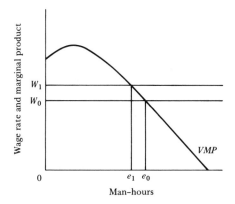

The corresponding line through C and D is the ridge line de-fined by moving vertically upward, with the number of man-hours fixed. Beyond it, for any fixed labor input, output cannot be in-creased by adding capital services. If instead we move from left to right along a line like the one at K_1, we start to the left of this upper ridge line, which marks the point where the average product of labor (output per man-hour) is at a maximum. No profit-maximizing entrepreneur would knowingly operate to the left of this point, since in this region he could always increase the output produced by a given labor input simply by not using all of his available inputs of capital. In other words, he is trying to man his equipment with such a small work force that he could increase output by leaving some equipment idle.

The peak of the marginal product schedule in Figure 7 must lie to the left of the point corresponding to the upper ridge line, since when average product is rising, marginal product must lie above it—that is, each additional man-hour must be pulling up the average. The marginal product schedule therefore slopes downward throughout the relevant range of input combinations between the two ridge lines. This downward slope represents the *law of variable proportions*, sometimes called the law of diminish-ing returns, which states that as one adds units of one factor to a fixed input of the other, the increments of product diminish.

If we assume that all units of product are sold at the same price, Figure 7 can be viewed as showing the value of the marginal product and can be used to show how the marginal productivity schedule in a particular production process determines the quantity of labor demanded in the short run. If the firm is confronted with the market wage W_0, it will employ e_0 man-hours. Wages and marginal product are both measured on the vertical axis of Figure 7. They can be expressed in the same units by either of two devices. The marginal product can be expressed in value terms by multi-plying it by the price of output per unit (where output is sold in a competitive market). Alternatively, one can imagine labor being paid in kind in output units, though this is unrealistic in a modern economy.

The value of total output is the area under the marginal product curve up to e_0. This whole area is divided into two parts: the wage bill (the rectangular area below W_0) and payments for capital services (the irregular area above W_0). Payments for capital services include depreciation charges, interest, and profit. In the case of fixed capital inputs, however, depreciation charges and interest charges will be insensitive to changes in wages or the amount of labor used; thus changes in the area representing payments to capital services can be viewed as changes in profit (that is, return on equity capital). The firm will not use more man-hours than e_0, because beyond this point the wage paid to hire another man-hour exceeds the value of its product; therefore adding labor reduces profits. If the market wage rose to W_1, the number of man-hours demanded would fall to e_1.

INTERPRETING THE SHORT-RUN DEMAND SCHEDULE

It should not be imagined that employers make explicit estimates of marginal product every time they hire a worker. Of course they do not. Most employers are not familiar with the term "marginal product." Yet they do make judgments about whether or not new employees are likely to be worth as much as they will cost, and many describe their decisions in these terms, which comes to very much the same thing.

Professor Fritz Machlup has suggested an analogy that is useful in this context. Imagine a driver deciding whether it is safe to overtake a truck on a two-lane road when a car is approaching in the opposite lane. A formal model of his decision involves several different elements, including the speed of the approaching car, how far away it is, the speed of the truck, the rate at which he can accelerate, and the condition of the road. He has neither the ability nor the time to estimate each element separately and to combine them in a formal analysis. Yet millions of such decisions are made intuitively every day—fortunately, correctly in the great majority of cases. Moreover, a formal model of the process might assist an analyst who was trying to design safer highways, even though it might not be a descriptively correct picture of the driver's conscious thoughts.

Critics of marginal productivity theory often assert that in the short run capital-labor ratios are fixed by technology, so that the short-run marginal product schedule is vertical and raising wages will therefore not reduce the use of labor. No doubt there are cases where this is true, but there are also many where it is not.

If one is using hand labor to dig a ditch and if one has only five shovels, each of which can be used by only one man at a time, it does not follow that the marginal product of a sixth man is zero. It has been fancifully suggested that the sixth man could contribute to output by fetching beer for the other five. More realistically, he could add to output by relieving each of the other five for ten minutes each hour, so that the shovels would always be in use while the men all rested regularly. Similarly, the speed of an automobile assembly line can be increased after relatively minor changes in equipment by adding more work stations and providing more relief workers to back up the line when the line workers fall behind or need rest.

The amount of labor used with a given kind of capital equipment cannot realistically be expected to vary in response to small changes in the wage rate. However, when one examines large differences in wages, such as those between developed and less developed countries, the possible range of manning practices for similar equipment is much more apparent.

In the United States a truck that delivers soft drinks to stores is usually operated by one man. I am told that in India similar trucks have a crew of four—a driver, a manager who keeps the records, and two porters who carry the cases into the store. This may well reflect appropriately the differences in the relative prices of labor and capital in the two countries. A similar but less extreme example is the contrast between the United States and Britain in the manning of city buses. Britain still (in 1970) has many two-man crews (driver and conductor) even on single-deck buses. Both the double-deck bus and the two-man crew disappeared more than 20 years ago in the United States, probably because of the high relative cost of labor. The case of the replacement of the double-deck bus, however, takes us away from the realm of fixed capital inputs and into the long run where capital inputs are variable.

THE DEMAND FOR LABOR IN THE LONG RUN

Figure 6 can also be used to derive the long-run demand for labor in a production process when technology is constant but the amount and nature of capital services used can be varied. The diagonal line tangent to Q_2 at E is a budget constraint representing a given sum to be spent in buying inputs. Its slope is determined by the ratio of the price of labor services to the price of capital services. The intercepts on the two axes show how much of each factor could be bought if the whole budget were devoted to buying that factor. The tangency at E indicates the long-run position of a cost-minimizing producer—at this point he would be getting the largest possible output for his fixed expenditure on inputs. Note that the condition that the producer be a cost minimizer is much weaker than the condition that he be a profit maximizer. It can reasonably be assumed that a government agency or a nonprofit institution will try to the best of its ability to minimize the costs of producing a given output.

Let us consider the case in which the price of labor is increased (with the price of capital services unchanged) and the budget is also increased to permit the production of the same output as before. The budget constraint line would still be tangent to Q_2 but would cut the horizontal axis further to the left. Its slope would be steeper and the point of tangency would lie further to the left. As equipment wore out, the producer would replace it with equipment designed to use less labor per unit of capital services. Since in the long run the substitution of capital for labor through changes in the amount and kind of capital equipment is possible, the long-run demand curve for labor must be more elastic than the short-run demand curve.

In the still longer run, one must abandon the assumption that the technology embodied in the production function is constant and unaffected by the wage rate. The direction of technological change can be influenced also by relative factor prices, with the greatest efforts being made to devise technologies that save the scarcest and most expensive inputs. It is this process that gives rise to the complaint that less developed countries, which import most of their technology from the developed world, are often saddled with technologies inappropriate to their factor endowments and would benefit from a technology that gave greater emphasis to saving capital.

For a given technology, the most widely used measure of the extent to which one input can be substituted for another is the elasticity of substitution, σ, which measures the percentage change in the ratio of factor inputs in response to a given small percentage change (of opposite sign) in the ratio of factor prices.[3] Note that σ is not the same as the marginal rate of substitution, the slope of the isoquant in Figure 6, which is measured in absolute rather than percentage units and measures the quantities of the factors rather than the ratio of quantities.

The elasticity of substitution is equal to zero if no substitution is possible; on an isoquant diagram this could be shown by drawing the isoquants L-shaped. It is infinitely large if the factors are perfect substitutes; this can be shown on an isoquant diagram by drawing the isoquants as straight lines. If the price ratio differs in slope from these straight isoquants, a cost-minimizing producer would use only the cheaper factor—that is, there would be a corner solution on one axis. Thus a small change in relative factor prices from one with the same slope as the isoquants to one with a slightly different slope would cause the denominator of the factor input ratio to go to zero, making the ratio indefinitely large. The case of perfect substitutes having different prices is not as far-fetched as it may seem at first. There may be many cases in which white labor and black labor with given training or experience are perfect substitutes in production, yet the black labor is cheaper. This implies, of coures, that where there is racial discrimination in wages, not all employers are profit maximizers—if they were, the differential would disappear. We shall return to this topic in Chapter 12.

Another special case of some interest is $\sigma = -1$, which occurs when a 1-percent change in the price ratio produces a 1-percent change in the opposite direction in the ratio of factor inputs. In this case the share of each factor in the total revenue will be constant despite changes in relative factor prices.

THE MARKET DEMAND SCHEDULE
AND MINIMUM-WAGE LAWS

Let us consider next how the demand for labor by firms can be used to derive a market demand schedule, still assuming that product prices are constant. The demand curve for labor by one firm is that shown in Figure 7, derived by multiplying the marginal physical product of labor by the product price to get the value of the marginal product. Each point on the curve shows the amount of labor the firm would employ at a given wage. To get the demand curve for a labor market, one would sum the demand curves of all the firms in the labor market horizontally. Since the curve for each firm slopes downward, the market demand curve must also slope downward. The intersection of this market demand curve and the upward-sloping supply curve of labor to this market would determine the equilibrium wage and the total number of man-hours worked. If wages were perfectly flexible, the equilibrium wage would always be the actual market wage. In fact, however, wages are not very flexible, so the market may not be in equilibrium following shifts in supply or demand.

A special case of prolonged disequilibrium is produced by the imposition of a legal minimum wage above the equilibrium wage. The theory of competitive labor markets predicts that such an effective minimum wage will reduce employment, as illustrated by the simple conventional analysis of Figure 8. For ease of exposition, in this figure employment is measured in men rather than man-hours; the analysis would be unchanged if man-hours were used instead.

The market demand curve is DD and the market supply curve is SS. Their intersection determines the competitive wage, W_c, at

FIGURE 8
The Effects of a Legal Minimum Wage
in a Competitive Market

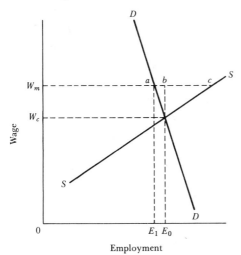

employment E_0. If a legal minimum wage is set at W_m, employment is reduced to E_1. The reduction in employment is smaller than the excess supply of labor at the minimum wage; the excess supply includes a second component consisting of workers who would like to work in this market at the new wage but are not hired. Some of these workers may be unemployed; others may be employed elsewhere at a lower wage. In the diagram the two components are shown by the horizontal distances *ab* and *bc*. The sizes of the two components depend on the slopes of the demand and supply schedules.

It should be noted that in the long run some of the reduction in employment may result from a reduction in the number of firms in the market rather than from changes in the number of workers employed by each firm. Such cases might occur where the firms in question competed, in the product market, with firms in other labor markets paying wages higher than W_m for superior labor. The minimum wage would then raise wages in the low-wage market without improving the quality of its labor. If the firms in question had been competing on even terms before the minimum-wage law, they would now be at a disadvantage and might have to move out of the local labor market or go out of business.

The formal analysis of a wage increase imposed on a competitive market by the formation of an effective trade union is, of course, the same as that for a legal minimum wage.

The effects of a minimum wage could be different under assumptions that depart from those of the competitive model. Some of the most important alternative models will be discussed in Chapter 5. It should be added that even under competitive conditions, the conclusion that a minimum-wage law will reduce employment does not dictate the judgement that such a law is undesirable. The gain in income to the remaining workers in the covered industries could be considered important enough to offset the losses to those who lose their jobs, particularly if some alternative source of income (including transfer payments) were available to the displaced workers.

Evidence of the reductions in employment predicted by competitive theory has been found in some careful statistical studies of the effects of minimum-wage laws.[4] When such studies are made by comparing conditions before and after the minimum wage is imposed or increased, it is important to make proper allowance for other factors affecting the level of employment during the interim. Thus in an industry in which employment had been expanding rapidly, one would not necessarily expect a reduction in employment to result from a minimum wage, but one would expect a smaller growth of employment in those areas or firms most affected by the legislation.

THE ROLE OF THE DEMAND
FOR THE FINAL PRODUCT

Although we began the discussion of the demand for labor in terms of the substitution between factors in production, that is by no means the only force involved. Since the demand for labor is derived from the demand for the products or services it produces, the nature of the demand for these final products or services is also of great importance. A shift in the demand for the final product will produce a shift in the same direction in the demand for the labor input, where a shift means a movement of the whole demand schedule to the right or left.

More interesting problems are presented by an increase in the wage of labor used in a particular industry relative to wages elsewhere. Frequently such wage increases occur where certain occupations are specialized to an industry, or where all the firms in an industry are covered by one collective bargaining agreement or by separate agreements with the same union. The impact of the wage increase on costs per unit of output will be minimized by substitution in production, but this will not ordinarily prevent some rise in unit costs, especially in the short run, when substantial changes in the input mix are seldom feasible. For a given wage increase, the size of the increase in unit costs depends not only on the elasticity of substitution but also on the importance of labor in the input mix—the larger the ratio of labor cost to other costs, the greater the increase in total unit costs. In a competitive industry it will also be true in the long run that none of the increase in total unit costs can be absorbed by profits; it will all be passed on in product prices. The impact of this price increase on the quantity of labor demanded will depend on the elasticity of demand for the final product.

Where the price elasticity of demand is small, the reduction in output and in the amount of labor demanded will also be small.

Price elasticity reflects the possibility of substitution in consumption. Like substitution in production, this will usually be less important in the short run than in the long, because substitution involves learning and may involve changes in capital equipment. Thus an increase in the relative wages of coal miners, passed on in the price of coal, would not immediately induce much change in the pattern of fuel consumption, since few users are equipped to burn more than one fuel. Over time, however, it would influence the type of fuel chosen for new installations and for the replacement of those that become obsolete.

The interaction of the elasticity of substitution, the elasticity of demand, and the share of a factor in the input mix is the subject of Marshall's famous four *laws of derived demand*, which were amended by Hicks. The demand for labor will be less elastic (1) the smaller the elasticity of substitution, (2) the smaller the elasticity of demand for the final product, (3) the smaller the initial ratio of labor cost to other costs, and (4) the less elastic the supply of the other factors. Hicks has demonstrated that for certain values of the elasticities of substitution and demand, proposition (3) is reversed. If the elasticity of substitution is greater than the elasticity of demand for the product, then the elasticity of demand for labor will be smaller, the *larger* the ratio of labor cost to other cost.[5] In other words, when the producer can substitute more easily than the consumer, it is an advantage to labor to have a large share in the initial input mix. In this case the use of labor is not much reduced by a rise in the product price, and substitution in production will be more difficult and expensive, the larger the amount of labor that needs to be replaced.

THE DEMAND FOR LABOR
IN THE ECONOMY AS A WHOLE

Having looked at the demand for labor in a firm and in an industry, we can now venture further and ask what the aggregate demand schedule for labor might look like—the curve showing the demand for labor in the economy as a whole. To construct such a curve, we must assume that all wages change in a constant proportion relative to some other input price, which we shall call the rate of interest. This is not the same as the price of capital services mentioned earlier, for that had two components: interest or its equivalent (such as normal profits on equity capital) and depreciation charges on capital goods. In the long run depreciation charges would rise with wages, though less than proportionally, as the higher costs of labor would be reflected in the prices of new capital goods. Nevertheless, a general rise in wages should lead to some long-run substitution of capital for labor, since it affects the whole of labor cost and only a portion of the cost of capital services.

We assume that the aggregate demand for all factors taken together remains unchanged. For example, this could happen if the change in relative factor prices consisted of an absolute increase in money wage and an absolute decrease in the rate of interest, such that the increased spending by wage earners was just matched by the decreased spending of interest receivers. Alternatively, one could think of the net effects on aggregate demand of a shift in relative prices as offset by a change in some exogenous factor, such as the level of government spending. This case should be contrasted with the usual case in macroeconomics in which an increase in the general level of wages is assumed to increase aggregate demand.

Our earlier discussion of substitution in consumption was based on a rise in wages in one industry only. This might lead one to think that if all wages rise together, there will be no substitution in consumption. This conclusion is not correct, however. Consider an example in which all wages rise by 10 percent and wages make up half the total costs of production in the coal industry but only one-fifth of the total costs of production in the petroleum industry. If, in the long run, cost increases are fully passed on in prices, the price of coal would rise 5 percent and that of fuel oil only 2 percent, leaving an incentive to use more fuel oil. This calculation ignores the labor cost component in the price of capital goods. To include it would alter the numbers but not the conclusion.

The argument of the last two paragraphs suggests that when all wages rise together, the force of substitution in both production and consumption is attenuated but still present. The aggregate demand curve for labor will therefore still slope downward, though it will be much less elastic than the demand curves for the great majority of particular uses defined in terms of relative wages.

We have now completed the treatment of the demand for labor under competition. In the next chapter we extend the treatment to other kinds of markets.

NOTES

1. For a good brief account of the historical development of marginal productivity theory and the criticism of it, see Allan M. Cartter, *The Theory of Wages and Employment* (Homewood, Ill.: Irwin, 1959), chaps. 2–4.
2. Alfred Marshall, *Principles of Economics*, 8th ed. (London: Macmillan, 1923), pp. 518–538.
3. For a mathematical definition and derivation of the elasticity of substitution, see J. R. Hicks, *The Theory of Wages*, 2d ed. (London: Macmillan, 1964), pp. 233–247 and 373–384.
4. See, for example, J. M. Peterson, "The Employment Effects of Minimum Wages," *Journal of Political Economy* 65 (1957), 412–430.
5. See Marshall, pp. 383–386; and Hicks, pp. 241–246.

The Demand for Labor: Some Extensions

THE DEMAND FOR LABOR
IN NONCOMPETITIVE PRODUCT MARKETS

The preceding chapter reviewed the theory of the demand for labor in perfectly competitive markets. In this chapter some of the assumptions of that discussion are relaxed to obtain propositions about demand in other circumstances. In particular, we examine the demand for labor in markets that are not perfectly competitive.

The simplest way to extend the competitive theory is to drop the assumption of perfect competition in product markets. Without perfect competition the firm faces a downward-sloping demand curve for its product. If it employs more labor, it must lower its product price to sell the additional output. In this case the demand curve for labor is not the value of the marginal product (marginal physical product $\times$ the product price), but *marginal revenue product, MRP* (marginal physical product $\times$ marginal revenue). Indeed, it is really the general case that labor is demanded up to the point where its wage is equal to the marginal revenue product, and perfect competition in product markets is a special case—in which marginal revenue product equals the value of the marginal product. Since in product markets that are not perfectly competitive marginal revenue is always less than price, marginal revenue product must always be less than the value of marginal product, and it will fall more rapidly as employment is increased.

If a profit-maximizing monopolist is confronted with a fixed wage, he will employ labor up to the point where the cost of another man-hour is equal to the marginal revenue product. In Figure 9, this is shown where the *MRP* curve cuts the wage, W_0, determining employment e_0. Beyond this point, using another man-hour would increase the wage bill more than it would increase total revenue, and would therefore reduce profits. The number of man-hours used will be less than in a competitive product market, and though labor will receive a wage equal to its marginal value to the firm, it will receive less than its marginal social product. This is not because its wage is lower than the wages of similar labor elsewhere, but because the restriction of output to maximize monopoly profit has raised the marginal social product of labor in this use above what it would be in a competitive product market.

FIGURE 9
The Demand for Labor in
a Noncompetitive Product Market

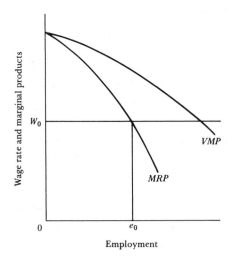

This is equally true of other factor inputs used by monopolists.

Although the analysis of the demand for labor by a profit-maximizing monopolist is a simple extension of marginal productivity theory, one may question whether real-world monopolists are typically profit maximizers in the short run. They may be under a variety of political and public-relations pressures to stabilize employment, to restrict profits to reasonable amounts, to restrain increases in product prices, and not to enlarge their share of the market unduly. The penalty for not complying with these pressures, or at least seeming to comply, could be government intervention to diminish or regulate their monopoly power. As a result, the management of a monopoly could choose to devote some monopoly profits to paying higher wages than the labor market requires or to using more labor than a profit maximizer would. In this case, high profits that might otherwise invite intervention are used to buy good labor relations and freedom from trouble.[1] Nevertheless, if such behavior is always present, an increase in wages might have effects on employment quite similar to those predicted by ordinary marginal analysis.

MONOPSONY IN LABOR MARKETS— THE FORMAL MODEL

From the point of view of labor theory, it is more interesting to abandon the assumption of competition in the labor market, restoring for simplicity the assumption of competition in product markets. The product market monopolist is confronted directly by the downward-sloping demand curve for his product rather than by a price set in a competitive product market. Similarly, the labor monopsonist is confronted directly by an upward-sloping supply curve of labor in his market rather than by a wage set in a competitive labor market.

Figure 10 shows the relevant schedules for a labor market monopsonist. The downward-sloping curve *VMP* is the *value of the marginal product*. The upward-sloping curve, *S*, is the supply curve of homogeneous labor, which in this case is measured in men rather than in man-hours. (The assumption that all men work the same number of hours avoids unnecessary complications in the subsequent discussion of discriminating monopsony.) The steeper

FIGURE 10
The Wage-Employment Position of a Monopsonist

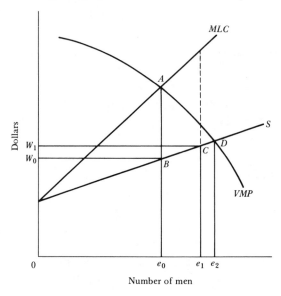

upward-sloping curve *MLC* is *marginal labor cost*, which measures the addition to the wage bill that results from employing an additional man when all men employed get the same wage (the case known as *nondiscriminating monopsony*). The upward-sloping supply curve indicates that new men can be hired only at wages above those paid to men already employed. The cost of hiring an additional man therefore includes both his own wage and the cost of bringing the wages of everyone previously employed up to the new level. For high levels of employment, the second element of this marginal cost can easily exceed the first. The profit-maximizing employment, e_0, is given by point A, where *MLC* and *VMP* are equal. Beyond this, employing another man adds more to total labor cost than it adds to total revenue. The wage corresponding to e_0, which is W_0, is given by the height of the supply curve at B.

Although Figure 10 is an extension of marginal productivity theory because the value of marginal product is one of the elements that determine the wage, the *VMP* curve in this case is *not* a demand curve for labor. The monopsonist has no demand curve for labor, in the sense of a simple functional relation in which quantity demanded depends on the wage, for exactly the same reason that a product market monopolist has no supply curve for his product. The number of men demanded depends not only on the height of the supply curve at any employment but also on its elasticity. Imagine another supply curve that also passes through B but slopes upward more steeply than S. The marginal-labor-cost curve corresponding to such a supply curve would lie above the one shown on Figure 10; employment would be lower than e_0 and the profit-maximizing wage would be determined at a point below W_0 on the new supply curve.

Figure 10 can be used to show that imposing a legal minimum wage on a monopsonist can sometimes increase employment. Suppose that the minimum wage is set at W_1. Marginal labor cost is equal to W_1 up to C, where W_1 crosses the supply curve. Up to that point additional men can be hired at the wage already being paid, and hiring them will add only their own wage to the wage bill. But at C there is a discontinuity in marginal labor cost, which jumps upward to the old MLC curve, as shown by the dotted line. The next man hired must be paid more than the minimum wage, and if he is hired, everyone previously employed must be paid more as well. If, as in this case, the VMP curve passes through the discontinuity, profit-maximizing employment will be e_1. By the same reasoning one can show that any minimum wage between A and B will increase employment. A minimum wage above A would decrease employment, as in the competitive case.

The employment of a perfectly discriminating monopsonist would be quite different from that of a nondiscriminator. By perfect discrimination we mean that the monopsonist is able to hire each man at his own supply price, thus paying unequal wages for equal work. Such an employer would maximize profit at D, with employment of e_2, which of course would also be the equilibrium employment of a perfectly competitive industry with the same supply and productivity conditions. But although the allocation of resources is the same in the two cases, the distribution of income is very different. In the competitive case, the wage bill is the rectangle whose northeast corner is at D and whose opposite corner is the origin. In the case of the discriminating monopsony, the triangular portion of this rectangle lying above the supply curve is part of profit.

The possibilities for paying different hourly wages, except through an incentive pay or piecework system, to different individuals doing the same work are probably quite limited for manual workers. There is among manual workers a strong tradition of concern about interpersonal equity, and there is general knowledge of rates of pay. Discriminating monopsony may be more possible for professional and managerial workers, where the tradition has been that salaries are confidential and related to individual merit, although this tradition may be beginning to break down. Where classes of equally productive workers, such as men and women, have different supply schedules, more limited kinds of discrimination are feasible. This problem, however, goes beyond the case of monopsony; it will be considered at length in Chapter 12.

MONOPSONY IN LABOR MARKETS— AN INTERPRETATION

Before an employer can be a discriminating monopsonist, he must first of all be a monopsonist. This takes us back to the question of how prevalent monopsony in labor markets actually is. There is some reason to think that the monopsony case has been given more attention in the literature than its actual importance would warrant.

The simplest case of monopsony is the company town with only one employer, a situation that was once common in the American textile and mining industries.[2] Today the importance of such cases is diminishing, both because they are found largely in declining industries and because better roads and the low cost of serviceable used cars have reduced the isolation of company towns. It is now practical and common for American workers to commute up to 25 miles to work, and very few employers provide the bulk of employment within a 25-mile radius of their establishments. The cost of commuting long distances leaves some residual monopsony power to isolated employers, but is less than where commuting is impossible.

The other possibility is collusive monopsony resulting from agreements among employers not to raise wages individually or not to hire away each other's employees. There is indeed evidence that some such agreements exist.[3] Except in the unusual case of professional sports, however, these agreements must be very difficult to enforce. They are not needed in loose labor markets, when there is no shortage of labor or upward pressure on wages.

When labor markets become tight, the temptation for the parties to collusive agreements to violate or evade them probably becomes irresistible. Once labor is scarce, it is in the interest of each employer to seek to raise the compensation of his workers relative to compensation elsewhere (for example, by allowing earnings to rise through upgrading, paying for unnecessary overtime, and similar devices), though he might maintain the agreed basic scale. Collusion among small numbers of employers is, of course, easier to establish and maintain than collusion among large numbers.

The employer who uses highly specialized workers is often the only employer in a labor market who employs workers in certain occupations. In this case, however, the monopoly power is bilateral. The workers have nowhere else to go without leaving the area, but the employer has no local labor supply beyond his own employees. If he attempts to exploit his position beyond obtaining a fair return on his investment in specialized training, the increased movement of his workers to other areas could produce losses on his past investment in them. A possible exception arises in the case of married women whose location may be determined by their husbands' employment.

Let us now return to the case in which an employer can hire all the workers he wants at the same wage, but let us abandon the assumption that they are all of equal quality and work equally hard. Instead, let us assume that the employer can rank his workers from best to worst, and that increasing his work force would mean adding workers less able than any now employed. The best workers would be the first hired and the last to be laid off. A short-run marginal product schedule drawn on these assumptions would be more steeply sloped downward than one that assumes homogeneous labor, since adding workers to the fixed input of capital now involves both raising the ratio of labor to capital inputs and lowering the quality of labor at the margin. Both forces work in the same direction. An increase in wages will still generally cause a reduction in employment, but it will be a smaller one than before.

This unrealistic case assumes a lack of competition in the market for ability and thus a total lack of bargaining power on the part of the superior workers. Their added ability or effort should command a premium over the wage of their less able or less energetic colleagues; the example assumes that the employer succeeds in capturing this rent for himself. Under fully competitive conditions all employers would be able to identify the abler workers, and the competition for them would raise their pay. This is what Marshall meant in arguing that competition would equalize not the time wages of workers in the same trade, but their efficiency wages—their wages relative to their abilities and efforts.[4] The tendency toward this result will of course be weaker, the greater the barriers to mobility and the greater the importance of seniority rules.

INTERDEPENDENCE BETWEEN WAGES AND PRODUCTIVITY

One of the assumptions involved in stating that wages are determined by the intersection of a supply curve with a demand curve based on marginal productivity is that the demand schedule is independent of the wage. If it were not, an upward shift of the supply schedule or an imposed increase in the wage rate would shift the position of the demand schedule, and the new equilibrium position would not lie on the old demand schedule. This assumption of independence has frequently been attacked by critics of marginal productivity theory. The criticism can be considered under two heads—cases in which wage increases raise the efficiency of workers, and cases in which wage increases improve the efficiency of management. The first is sometimes called *the economy of high wages* and the second is sometimes called *shock theory*. The possible relation between wages and the supply of effort by way of better nutrition and health was mentioned in Chapter 2, where it was suggested that the effect is probably not of any substantial importance in developed countries. However, since the analysis may be of practical importance in less-developed countries and is in any case of some theoretical interest, it is worth while to try to construct a demand schedule under these assumptions. This is done in Figure 11, which shows the demand for labor by a firm.

The analysis assumes that instead of a single marginal productivity curve there is a family of such curves, one for each wage, with higher wages corresponding to higher marginal productivity schedules. The demand curve, *D*, then connects the points at which each wage crosses its own marginal productivity schedule, at points

FIGURE 11
The Economy of High Wages

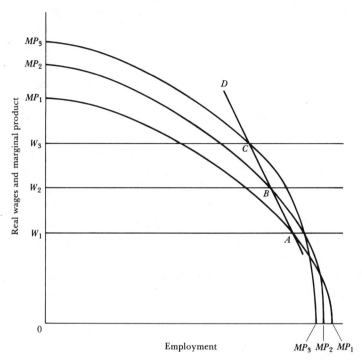

such as *A*, *B*, and *C*. The demand curve is steeper than any of the marginal productivity curves at the points where it crosses them, since the marginal productivity curves for higher wages must lie above those for lower ones. Thus under conditions where productivity increases with the level of wages, the reduction in employment induced by wage increases will be smaller than it would be along a demand curve based on a single marginal product schedule.

The wages chosen for illustration in Figure 11 differ by constant amounts. The corresponding increments in product have been drawn so that they are always smaller than the increments in wages.[5] This assumes that the worker is not a perfectly efficient machine for converting higher wages into added product, if only because he will normally share his wages with his family and will spend some of them on consumption that does not raise efficiency. An employer would not continue a situation in which output could be increased more than proportionately by increasing wages unless he did so from ignorance. Even a slave owner would spend more in feeding his slaves if he knew that their product would rise by more than the added outlay. Only casual labor markets might produce exceptions to the requirement that productivity cannot rise more than in proportion to wages except through ignorance. If no employer hires the same workers from day to day, one employer's high wages would contribute to increasing the output produced by other employers, and not to increasing the output of his own firm.

The vertical distance between successive marginal product curves in Figure 11 decreases as wages rise, indicating that successive increments in wages have diminishing returns in added product. The marginal product curves also converge as employment increases, and eventually they cross. This indicates that, with the quantity of other factors fixed, the amount of labor (in efficiency units) needed to bring total product to a maximum (or marginal product to zero) is embodied in a smaller number of men when the wage is high. If we assume, for example, that ten poorly paid men working for a week could cultivate a field so thoroughly that further cultivation would not increase its output, the same point might be reached in a week by eight well-paid men.

The analysis of shock theory is not unlike that of the economy of high wages, except that it is management's productivity that is said to increase with the wage rate. This difference makes the shock theory applicable to developed countries. The theory is often used to argue that there need be no reduction in employment in response to a wage increase (that is, that the demand curve for labor is vertical); this argument is usually restricted to cases in which large increments in wages are imposed on the firm by unions or by minimum-wage laws. Such large wage increases, or shocks, are contrasted with the more gradual changes in wages that might be required by the tightening of a competitive market.

The basic premise of shock theory is that any organization operates with some slack or inefficiency and that this inefficiency can be reduced when the organization is seriously threatened. This will produce a higher marginal productivity schedule for labor in response to a sudden wage increase, since special attention will be given to eliminating inefficiency in the use of the factor whose price has suddenly increased.

It is important to note that one cannot confirm shock theory merely by observing that the result of a wage increase is the use of more or newer machinery per unit of labor. Such changes are exactly what is predicted by the marginal productivity explanation of demand and are represented by a movement to the left along the old marginal productivity curve. Shock theory requires that there be a new marginal productivity curve lying above the old one, produced by some innovation in techniques or organization.

Shock theory is most plausible as applied to the unionization of a previously nonunion enterprise. In most cases this will produce both a substantial wage increase and a simultaneous challenge to the unlimited authority of management and its ways of doing things, which could well inspire management to reexamine its methods and procedures with some care. It is much harder to imagine repeated waves of successful innovation in response to annual wage increases negotiated with an established union. Such negotiated wage increases will themselves become routine, and a complacent organization can deal inefficiently with them as well as with other aspects of its activity.

FIXED COSTS
OF EMPLOYMENT

So far in the discussion of demand we have been assuming that the cost of labor to the employer consists only of an hourly wage. We now drop that assumption and recognize that there are also fixed costs of employment.[6] These fixed costs have important implications for the incidence of unemployment by skill level and for the employer's choices between changes in numbers of workers and changes in hours of work.

Broadly defined, fixed costs of employment are any costs that vary less than proportionately with the hours worked by an individual employee. These costs are of two general types. The first are turnover costs—the costs incurred when employees are hired, laid off, or discharged. These include the costs of recruitment, screening, and initial training, as well as such terminal costs as severance pay and increases in taxes for unemployment insurance. The second type of fixed costs consists of costs that occur throughout the period of employment but are not related (or not fully related) to hours of work. A tax on employment based on numbers of employees rather than on wages or man-hours, or any payroll tax whose tax base has an annual earnings limit, would fall in this category. So would similarly based contributions to private pension and welfare plans.

It is important to avoid the incorrect generalization that all fringe benefits are fixed costs; whether they are or not depends on the details of how they are calculated. For example, contributions to a health and welfare fund stated in dollars per employee per month involve an element of fixed costs, since they are not increased by overtime work. Contributions stated as a percentage of payroll, including overtime pay, would have quite an opposite effect, since if overtime were paid for at premium rates, the contribution would in effect also be paid at premium rates. The neutral case is that in which the contribution is paid at the same rate for standard and overtime hours.

For several reasons turnover cost rises as a proportion of total labor cost with the skill level of the employee. Much more intensive search is involved in hiring highly skilled employees such as professionals or executives than in hiring unskilled workers. Expenses for recruiting, including agency fees or advertising, and for screening will be higher for the skilled employee. Expenses for travel to interviews may be paid; references will be checked more carefully; more expensive management time will be used in interviewing. This is because in jobs that involve great responsibility, mistakes in staffing can be very costly. Although there are few data available on the costs of hiring, those shown in Table 9 support the general conclusions just stated.

Training costs as well as hiring costs usually vary with skill level since the period of induction or specialized on-the-job training needed before the new employee reaches his full usefulness will usually be longer for more skilled workers. A new janitor might be fully effective by his second or third day in the job; a new executive might need months to learn all he needs to know about how an organization functions.

Differences in fixed costs by level of skill imply that employers will be more reluctant to lay off skilled than unskilled employees, especially in response to a drop in demand that is expected to be temporary. The longer an employee remains with an employer, the longer the period over which the initial fixed costs can be amortized. To lay off a skilled employee in response to a temporary reduction in demand frequently involves incurring new fixed costs when demand revives, for the employee on layoff may find suitable

TABLE 9

Average Hiring Costs by Occupation and Industry,
Monroe County, New York, 1965–1966[a]

Occupation Group	Manufacturing	Nonmanufacturing
Professional, managerial, and technical	$1139	$292
Clerical	150	130
Skilled manual	537	103
Semiskilled and unskilled	92	94
All occupations	222	138

[a] The data were obtained from a survey of 17 employers in the Rochester, New York, area.

Source: John G. Myers, *Job Vacancies in the Firm and the Labor Market*, Studies in Business Economics No. 109, National Industrial Conference Board, Table 3-1, p. 31.

work elsewhere and not return to his former work when he is recalled. Thus the existence of fixed costs in large part explains the greater stability of employment and lower unemployment rates of skilled workers.

The most conspicuous distinction in the stability of employment is that between manual and white-collar workers. The former are usually hired by the hour and the latter by the month or year, and longer notice of layoff or dismissal is typically given to white-collar employees. If demand falls, all white-collar employees may be permitted to continue to work at a less-intensive pace, while some blue-collar employees are usually laid off. Since on average the white-collar employees have a higher level of skill, the fixed-cost concept has some relevance to these differences in treatment. Yet there is much overlap in levels of skill between the two broad classes of workers—for example, skilled craftsmen are better paid and have a longer period of training than many clerical workers. This may suggest that the higher level white-collar skills are more specific to particular firms. But it also suggests that there is a quite different basis for the differences in treatment between manual and white-collar workers—one more rooted in the concept of social class than in the economics of overhead costs.

When, despite a drop in demand, an employer retains a worker because he has a substantial investment in him, he is usually paying the worker more than his *current* marginal product. The decision to retain the worker involves the judgment that over some longer period his marginal product will exceed his wage, even though it is lower at the moment. We use the word "exceed" rather than "equal" because the current deficit must be made up. It is irrelevant, however, whether or not the initial investment in the worker has been fully amortized. That is now a sunk cost, and unless in the future the worker's marginal product is expected to exceed his wage, unrecovered initial investment is lost in either case (dismissal or retention).

The fixed costs of employment not only restrain employers from laying workers off but also give rise to losses from voluntary turnover. As Becker has pointed out, in the traditional model of demand it makes no difference whether an employer hires the same workers indefinitely or different ones each day.[7] This is one of the implications of the assumptions of homogeneous labor and the absence of hiring costs—they do not permit one to distinguish between a casual market, such as the market for day-haul workers to harvest fruit or vegetables, and more typical labor markets. The introduction of fixed costs, particularly specific training, means that new employees are imperfect substitutes for present employees. Employers therefore try to reduce voluntary quits by a variety of devices that make seniority a valuable right and reduce quits by experienced workers. Vacation and pension benefits are related to length of service. Layoffs are almost always made in reverse order of seniority so that senior employees have greater job security. Higher-level jobs are filled by promotion from below, with seniority given weight in the selection for promotion.

This way of looking at seniority rights as beneficial to management may surprise some who view them as inventions of unions. Unions and workers favor seniority on grounds of equity and because they do not trust management to apply other criteria, such as ability, in an objective way. The unions therefore tend to get customary seniority rights embodied in written agreements and try to increase the weight given to seniority in promotion. But the interests of union and management conflict only to the extent that seniority and ability are uncorrelated; where experience with an employer is valuable, the correlation is often high.

The practice of promotion from within based heavily on seniority is particularly important among blue-collar workers. In some industries, such as basic steel and petroleum refining, long chains of progression extending into highly skilled jobs are filled in this way, and training for each job takes place through working at the next lower job. In such cases the firm hires from the external labor market only at the lowest-level job, or *port of entry*. Other jobs are filled and rewarded through the operation of the *internal labor market*.[8] The absence of external markets in the skills specific to these industries protects the employer's investment in on-the-job training; job security and high pay at the top of the promotion ladder reward the senior employee and help induce entry at the bottom.

The importance of fixed costs helps us understand a divergence of views between economists and managers on the value of voluntary mobility. The traditional model of economists views with approval the worker who quits his job to gain a slight advantage. Such mobility creates the competitive labor market that tends to insure that workers are used where they are most needed by the economy. Employers, however, have generally regarded voluntary turnover as an evil to be combatted. Since by definition there cannot be a highly competitive market for workers with specific training, one is inclined to sympathize with employer efforts to reduce turnover and to minimize fixed costs of employment per man-hour by spreading them over a long job tenure. However, specific training automatically creates a deterrent to quits by making the worker's value higher to his present employer than to others, provided only that the worker gets a wage that reflects this value (net of the employer's costs of training, including interest). Thus there may not be any need for additional devices, such as nonvested pensions, to "tie" the worker to his job.

The increasing importance of fixed costs of employment also helps to explain the rapid growth in recent years of temporary-help agencies. Such agencies provide employers with clerical workers or laborers on a day-to-day basis to meet unusual needs or to replace workers who are absent. The employer pays an hourly rate above that prevailing for permanent employees but bears none of the costs of recruiting, screening, payroll accounting, and payroll taxes—all of which are paid by the agency. The workers gets a substantially lower wage rate than that paid by the employer, with the difference providing for the fixed costs and the agency's profit margin. Working for temporary-help agencies is especially attractive to workers who for some reason are not available for long periods of work—for example, transients, people with health problems, and pregnant women.[9]

THE DEMAND
FOR OVERTIME HOURS

Let us now consider the choices of an employer whose workers are already working the standard workweek and who, because of an increase in the demand for his product, wants to use more labor. He can do so either by hiring more men or by working his present work force overtime. Working longer hours will involve paying for overtime at premium rates and may also involve losses of efficiency resulting from fatigue, increased absenteeism, and a larger amount of leisure taken on the job. Hiring more men involves the fixed costs of recruitment, screening, and training. These costs will be greatly reduced if the employer already has experienced former employees on layoff. Adding men also increases fixed elements of compensation, such as social security taxes, which do not increase with hours worked beyond some limit. These fixed elements make the true overtime premium smaller than the stated one. Although the premium is 50 percent of the hourly wage, it is usually less than 50 percent of total compensation per man-hour. Finally, if the plant is already fully in use during the original working hours, hiring more men may involve adding equipment or redesigning work places so that more men can be used with existing equipment.

If a plant is not being used all the hours of the week, adding hours will not usually involve changing the ratio of labor to capital inputs in any important way. Added man-hours and machine-hours will be used in the usual proportions. The added machine-hours will have little extra cost; it will consist largely of additional maintenance and the portion of depreciation that depends on use. Adding men, however, increases the ratio of labor to capital inputs during the hours already worked and is subject to diminishing returns in the usual sense.

The choice between adding men and adding hours also depends on the quality of the workers available in the market, and depends heavily on how long the increase in demand is expected to last. If the increase is expected to be temporary, the cost of hiring men and laying them off again will usually be viewed as prohibitive, and overtime will usually be worked. Some aspects of these costs may be quite indirect. An employer whose employment is very unstable may acquire a bad reputation that could hamper recruitment or even hurt sales. Employers with a strong social conscience might incur psychic costs in choosing an unstable employment strategy.

The element of overtime cost that results from fatigue and absenteeism rather than from the wage premium will also be smaller when overtime is temporary. The longer the increase in demand is expected to last, the smaller the fixed costs become, relative to the cost of overtime, and the stronger is the case for adding men. This reasoning explains the consistent tendency of changes in hours of work to occur before changes in employment at cyclical turning points. Hours are increased or decreased when employers are still uncertain about the strength of changes in demand; employment is changed in the same direction once the importance of the demand shift has become clear.[10]

During the postwar period there has been a tendency for the amount of overtime work to increase. One possible explanation for this is that the fixed costs of employment may have become larger relative to premiums for overtime work, which have generally been constant. Since fixed costs are more important for skilled than for unskilled employees, the rising average level of skill contributes to the rise in the importance of fixed costs.

The position of the employer is not very different when he is faced with a decrease in demand rather than an increase. The costs of separation and rehiring will lead him to prefer shorter hours. This will be particularly true if he is paying for overtime initially, since he will save the overtime premium. The barrier to reducing hours much below the standard workweek lies in the attitudes of the workers. Senior workers will prefer to have junior workers laid off rather than suffer lower weekly earnings themselves. An adequate system of unemployment insurance also strengthens the case (from the workers' standpoint) for maintaining a normal workweek, though the most prevalent method of financing such insurance, which relates the employer's taxes to claims for benefits by his own former employees, increases the employer's incentive to shorten hours instead. The expected duration of the drop in demand again plays its part. Reductions in hours are much more likely to be used where the decrease in demand is expected to be temporary.

White-collar employees are usually guaranteed a full work-week even in the face of decreases in the work load. At the highest levels, there is some offset to the costs of this guarantee in cases where employees are expcted to work extra hours under special circumstances without additional compensation. The annual salary of an executive or a professional worker is thus entirely a fixed cost. It can be reduced only by dismissing the employee, and at this level dismissals are not common. The growing ratio of salaried to hourly paid workers suggests that fixed costs of employment will become even more important in the future than they are now. This leads us to conclude that of all the modifications of the traditional theory of the demand for labor in competitive markets, the introduction of the concept of fixed costs is the most important.

NOTES

1. For an elaboration of this point, see J. R. Monson, Jr. and A. Downs, "A Theory of Large Managerial Firms," *Journal of Political Economy* 73 (June 1965), 221–236.
2. There has been very little study of the amount of employer concentration in labor markets. A leading study is Robert L. Bunting, *Employer Concentration in Local Labor Markets* (Chapel Hill: University of North Carolina Press, 1962).
3. See, for example, Richard A. Lester, *Adjustments to Labor Shortages* (Princeton, N.J.: Industrial Relations Section, 1955), pp. 46–49.
4. Alfred Marshall, *Principles of Economics*, 8th ed. (London: Macmillan, 1923), p. 547. For an attempt to measure the relation between individual wages and ability, see A. Rees and G. P. Shultz, *Workers and Wages in an Urban Labor Market* (Chicago: University of Chicago Press, 1970), pp. 88–90.
5. In terms of the diagram, this requires that the area between two marginal product curves up to any given employment must be less than the area between the corresponding wage levels. This condition is ordinarily sufficient to insure that the demand curve slopes backward. For an analysis that violates it, giving a forward-sloping demand curve, see Richard Perlman, *Labor Theory* (New York: Wiley, 1969), pp. 50–56. The condition is also violated in Harvey Leibenstein, "The Theory of Underemployment in Backward Economies," *Journal of Political Economy* 65 (April 1957), 91–103. This is one of the earliest and most complete discussions of the economy of high wages.
6. One of the earliest and most complete discussions of the issues treated in this section is Walter Y. Oi, "Labor as a Quasi-Fixed Factor," *Journal of Political Economy* 70 (December 1962), 538–555.
7. Gary S. Becker, *Human Capital: A Theoretical and Empirical Analysis, with Special Reference to Education* (New York: National Bureau of Economic Research, 1964), p. 21.
8. The terms *port of entry* and *internal labor market* have been introduced into the literature by John T. Dunlop. For an extensive development of these concepts, see Peter B. Doeringer and Michael Piore, *Internal Labor Markets and Manpower Analysis* (Lexington, Mass.: Heath, 1971).

9. For a more detailed account of the development of temporary-help agencies, see Mack A. Moore, "Historical Development, Operation, and Scope of the Temporary Help Service Industry," *Industrial and Labor Relations Review* (July 1965).
10. For evidence of this, see Gerhard Bry, *The Average Workweek as an Economic Indicator*, Occasional Paper 69 (National Bureau of Economic Research, 1959).

PART III

Labor Markets and Labor Mobility

Job Search, Mobility, and Migration

THE SEARCH PROCESS

The analysis of many markets can safely be confined to the forces that determine supply and demand, and little attention need be paid to the mechanics of the market itself. This is not true of labor markets, however. Because wages are unusually rigid, sticky prices (especially downward) labor markets do not ordinarily clear; that is, quantity supplied is not ordinarily equal to quantity demanded. Quantity supplied is composed of two distinct parts, employment and unemployment; and quantity demanded also consists of two parts, employment and unfilled job vacancies. The forces governing the total quantities, discussed in Parts I and II, are not identical with the forces that govern these divisions, which remain to be discussed. We begin that task in this chapter by discussing the process of search by individual workers and employers, and we shall continue it in the next chapter with a more aggregative view of unemployment and vacancies.

Standardized goods or securities are often traded in organized markets, such as stock or commodities exchanges, where prices fluctuate freely so as to clear the market at all times. Markets for less homogeneous commodities or services are characterized in varying degree by differences in the prices asked or offered by different sellers or buyers at a given time; there are also differences in quality or terms of sale that correspond in part to these price differences. Participants in such markets must engage in search in order to get good terms.

Search takes place in labor markets for two main reasons. First, even within one occupation there are many important differences among both workers and jobs. These differences are complex, multidimensional, and often difficult to quantify or to describe. Second, the fixed costs of employment discussed in Chapter 5 insure that in most cases a person holds a job for a substantial period of time. A hiring transaction is therefore a large transaction for both parties, more like buying a car than like buying a loaf of bread; for the worker the transaction is one that is not frequently repeated. A large, nonrecurring transaction will involve more search than a small, frequent one. It requires new search on each occasion, since what has been learned in looking for one's last job is usually not still relevant. Moreover, the absolute differences in terms offered by different sellers or buyers may be large, justifying substantial outlays on search in order to improve the terms of the transaction.

Consider the case of an experienced unemployed worker who is looking for a job in his usual occupation. A number of employers may be hiring workers with his competence and offering different wages. If he accepts the first offer he receives, he is unlikely to be making the best possible bargain. He will therefore look into a number of possibilities—a process that involves costs. The most important of these costs is his own time; by prolonging his period of unemployment to search further he sacrifices the income he could have earned during the search period, less any unemployment insurance benefits to which he is entitled. He may also incur direct costs such as carfare, postage, employment-agency fees, or the cost of placing an advertisement in a newspaper. These costs represent an investment on which the expected return is the present value of the difference in compensation between the first job offer he receives and the one that is finally accepted.

The search begins with the most promising possibilities, such as firms known to pay good wages and the establishments closest to the worker's home. As the number of openings investigated increases, the probability decreases that a new offer will be better than any previously received. Eventually the worker concludes that the probable gain from further search is less than the additional cost, and he accepts the best previous offer still open. This is not necessarily the last offer he has received. In the light of the information obtained from continued search, it may appear that an earlier offer is in fact the best available, and the worker may return to it.

One of the less-tangible costs of continued search is that opportunities already discovered may be taken by others if they are not accepted quickly and will be gone if the worker should decide to return to them. The higher the level of unemployment in the area or occupation, the greater is this risk. If unemployment is very high, a worker may accept the first offer he receives, thinking it unlikely that he will get a better one and very likely that this opening will be promptly filled by someone else if he does not accept it at once. Under these circumstances he may also have to search for some time before he receives any offer at all. Thus the amount and duration of *frictional unemployment*—the unemployment generated by the search process—are not independent of the general level of demand for labor.

Of course, not all the workers who look for jobs are unemployed. A worker who is dissatisfied with his job for any reason may look for a better position while still holding his present one. The principal cost of search in this case is the loss of leisure time rather than the loss of employment income, and this cost will generally be lower. The worker may discover that he cannot improve his position and will stay on his present job, or he may move with no intervening period of unemployment.

In assessing the job offers he receives, the worker is interested in far more than the wage. He is interested in job security, the costs of commuting, opportunities for advancement, fringe benefits, interesting work, congenial colleagues, and many similar factors. He will therefore not necessarily choose the job that offers the highest starting wage. Even where money wages are very important to him, a lower starting wage may be offset by better opportunities for wage increases or promotion.

This account has implicitly assumed that the unemployed

worker comes into the market with no particular ideas about his worth, and that he forms such ideas from the offers that are made to him. An alternative view may usually be closer to the truth —that the worker enters the market with strong notions of what he wants, based on his pay in his last job and general information obtained from friends and relatives. These notions are the basis of a reservation price—the lowest wage he will initially consider—which he revises downward in the light of the offers he receives until he becomes willing to accept one.[1] At the same time, employers with vacancies to fill are also engaged in search. If they find vacancies hard to fill at the wages they initially offer, they will improve their wage offers or lower their hiring standards until the vacancies can be filled. The search process thus produces an accommodation between the originally incompatible aspirations of workers and requirements of employers, both of which are modified through time to become more and more realistic. This does not mean that the parties to a given hiring transaction must have been searching for the same length of time. Nothing precludes a newly unemployed worker from accepting a job that has been vacant for some time, nor an employer from hiring a long-unemployed worker for a vacancy that has just occurred.

Large employers hiring for occupations in which they employ substantial numbers of people are less likely to change their wage offers in response to information obtained in the search process. Often their wage level is set by collective bargaining or by company policy over which personnel managers in particular plants have no control. In these cases, if vacancies are hard to fill, the adjustments will be made entirely by widening the area of search, by using more costly methods of search, or by lowering hiring standards and applying them more flexibly.

The employer who offers low wages will have to search longer and harder than the employer who offers high wages, and he will often have to use more expensive channels of recruiting.[2] The high-wage employer can choose among many good applicants, who may present themselves as soon as it becomes known that he is hiring. Thus high-wage costs are to some extent offset by lower costs of recruitment, screening, and training. But there is no reason to expect the offset to be complete, particularly where the high-wage employers are required by collective bargaining agreements to pay more than they would choose to pay in the absence of unions.

Just as workers consider opportunities for promotion in deciding which offers to accept, employers must consider suitability for promotion in selecting new employees. In hiring for a "dead end" job, only the applicant's ability to perform the initial job need be considered. But where a job is the first step in a promotional ladder, the employer will select the workers who seem to have the most potential for advancement.

Like the worker, the employer must decide how long to continue his search. If none of the applicants for an opening quite measures up to his standards, he must weigh the cost of relaxing the standards against both the costs of securing additional applications and those of keeping the vacancy unfilled. The latter costs may include lost output or the costs of overtime payments to his present workers. If the probability of getting better applicants seems small and the costs of keeping the job vacant are high, he will take the best of the applicants still available, which need not be the one who applied last. The lower the unemployment rate, the greater will be the probable cost of rejecting an applicant in the hope of finding a better one.

An employer who has decided to search outside his own organization to fill a vacancy above the starting level may eventually decide instead to fill the position by promotion from within, thus creating a new vacancy at a lower level. If he fills a vacancy by hiring a man already employed elsewhere, a new vacancy will usually be created in another firm. Thus the filling of a vacancy at a high level can lead to a chain of mobility, internal or external to the firm, ending when a vacancy in the chain is filled by someone not already employed. And even this person need not be unemployed—he could be a new entrant to the labor force. It should therefore be kept in mind that the common description of the search process as "matching unfilled vacancies with unemployed men" is in fact an oversimplification.

CHANNELS OF EMPLOYMENT

The process of search in labor markets takes place through a number of channels of employment, formal and informal, whose importance varies from place to place and by type of job. The informal channels include referrals from present employees and *gate hiring*—applications in response to a notice of a vacancy posted on an employer's premises, such as a sign in a restaurant window, "waitress wanted" or "dishwasher wanted." The least formal method of all is the walk-in, the application not solicited in any way. The principal formal channels are the public employment service, private employment agencies, newspaper advertisements, schools, and union hiring halls.

Informal channels are by far the most important for unskilled and semiskilled blue-collar occupations. Firms paying better than average wages or firms in markets where there is substantial unemployment can usually fill all their vacancies through referrals by present workers and through unsolicited applications. This method is unsystematic, because it fails to reach the largest number of potential applicants. However, employee referrals have a variety of advantages to both the employer and the applicant. The employer gets some amount of screening from the referring employee, whose own reputation is involved and who is therefore unlikely to refer an applicant he knows to be clearly unsuitable. At the same time, the applicant gets from his friend detailed information about working conditions and supervisory practices, which he cannot get through formal sources. He would probably distrust information of this kind if it were provided by the employer or an employment agency. If the applicant is hired, he has a friend in the establishment to help make him feel at home and to show him how things are done.

Among formal sources, the public employment service has two great advantages. It charges no fees to either the employer or the employee, and it generally has the largest pool of information about unemployed workers and job vacancies. These advantages should give it a more central role in the labor market than it has yet attained. One of its handicaps has been that the long and close association of the employment service with the unemployment insurance program has tarnished its image for skilled and white-collar workers, and for some employers, who feel that the service is more interested in placing the insured unemployed than in meeting the employer's requirements. Another important difficulty may be that the available information on job openings and applicants cannot be scanned quickly and thoroughly enough by the methods now in use, which consist largely of the manual search of files. Computerization of the public employment service, which is still in the exploratory stages, could greatly improve the position of the service. A computerized service could locate for each client the four or five vacancies or applicants of all those in the files that come closest to meeting a set of specific requirements. Even with computerization, however, the public employment service is unlikely to displace employee referral as the most important channel of employment, because of the great advantage of employee referral in transmitting trustworthy qualitative information.

Private employment agencies are of greatest importance in white-collar markets in large cities. Most small labor markets do not generate enough transactions to support a private agency; in such markets the public employment service is more likely to make a substantial share of white-collar placements. A conspicuous characteristic of the private agencies is their willingness to make substantial expenditures on advertising to attract applicants. Furthermore, in private agencies the payment of counselors on a commission basis gives the staff a strong incentive to make placements, although it sometimes encourages unethical practices such as attempting to recruit workers previously placed.

The fee structure of private employment agencies offers clues to the way in which costs of search vary with skill level and are distributed between buyers and sellers. Agency fees tend to be a higher fraction of the wage or salary, the higher the level of the job, with the highest percentage rates charged by professional and executive agencies. Thus costs of search seem to rise more than in proportion to salary levels. Agency fees are generally paid by employers in markets where there are many unfilled vacancies, such as clerical markets, and by employees in markets where there are many unemployed workers, such as the market for unskilled male labor.

Newspaper advertisements, used mostly by employers, reach a wide audience at relatively low cost but produce a flow of unscreened applicants. They are therefore used mostly in markets where labor is scarce and by large employers with personnel departments that can carry out screening. Some amount of preselection can be achieved by careful choice of newspapers. For example, employers who want to recruit blacks advertise in black newspapers, while those who discriminate against them often use neighborhood papers in all-white neighborhoods.

Increasing the efficiency of labor-market intermediaries will shift more of the search process from informal to formal channels and reduce the total cost of search. The benefits could come in the form of a reduced volume of frictional unemployment or in a better matching of job seekers and vacancies, resulting in improved job satisfaction and performance.

VOLUNTARY MOBILITY

Workers sometimes change jobs because they must—because they have been dismissed for misconduct or poor performance or have been made superfluous by technological change or shifts in demand. Other workers choose to change jobs because they are dissatisfied with their present ones or expect to do better elsewhere. The first kind of mobility, *involuntary mobility*, often forces the worker to take a job that pays less than his previous one, whereas *voluntary mobility* generally results in an improvement of the worker's position. Our present concern is with the costs of voluntary mobility and the returns to it.

If all labor markets were in equilibrium, voluntary mobility would occur only when one set of jobs became more attractive through a rise in its relative wages or an improvement in its nonpecuniary advantages. Such changes would induce a flow of labor toward the jobs that had become more attractive. However, as we have stressed earlier, labor markets are usually not in equilibrium. For many jobs the compensation is above that needed to attract recruits and there is ordinarily an excess supply of applicants, many of whom are already employed at less-attractive jobs. Such situations result from high wages set through collective bargaining or from declines in demand where wages are rigid downward, as they usually are.

In such cases voluntary mobility will occur whenever there are openings in the high-wage jobs, without the need for further improvement in their relative wage. Similarly, migration to high-wage cities or regions is stimulated by a low level of unemployment in these areas and the increased hiring of unskilled labor, without the need for any widening of geographic wage differentials.

A worker who changes jobs can change his location, his occupation, his industry, his employer, or any combination of these. Particular kinds of moves are characteristic of different kinds of workers. An unskilled worker many change his occupation frequently, working first as a dishwasher, then as a laborer, then as a messenger. Clearly a skilled worker would not voluntarily make such shifts, for he would earn much less if he worked outside his usual trade. Nevertheless, there are a few common patterns of occupational change among the highly skilled, particularly the shift of lawyers, engineers, and accountants into management. Such shifts are usually made without changing employers and may involve a very gradual change of duties and responsibilities.

Although the professional or managerial worker is much less likely to change his occupation than is the unskilled worker, he is much more likely to change location. In a highly specialized field it is often impossible to change employers without moving some distance, and markets for specialized skills are often national or even international. Semiskilled workers, on the other hand, have very firm attachments to their communities, perhaps because they get less of their satisfactions from their work and more from social life based on contacts with their neighbors. Firms offering geographical transfer rights to operatives in plants that have closed have discovered that unless the way is carefully paved, few workers will agree to move. They often prefer to accept a high risk of remaining unemployed for a long while rather than move a few hundred miles to a strange community.[3]

Mobility among industries depends very much on whether a worker's occupation is specialized to an industry. A truck driver can change industries very easily, since firms in diverse industries may use the same kind of truck. A roller in a steel mill, on the other hand, could not change industries without a large loss of income, though he might change employers if a new mill opened in his area. Where skills are specialized to one employer, voluntary mobility will be extremely low, and a worker may spend his entire career with the same employer.

Perhaps the most firmly established fact about voluntary mobility of all kinds is that it declines sharply with age, both because the psychic costs of moving rise with age and because the remaining length of working life sets an outer limit on the period during which returns can be received. The natural impediments to voluntary mobility of older workers created by family responsibilities and the decline of the spirit of adventure are reinforced by the growth of specialized skills and by seniority rights and non-vested pensions. When an older worker loses his job in a plant shutdown or because of technical change, he may be forced to accept a new job that requires far less skill or is much lower paid. For some older workers early retirement is preferable to retraining or relocation. In part this solution is chosen because it is harder to "teach an old dog new tricks" (though not impossible, as the proverb would have it); in part it is chosen because there is not enough time left in which to perform them.

MIGRATION

The sorts of issues raised in the study of labor mobility can be illustrated by considering the case of geographic mobility, or migration, in more detail. The migration of labor is a somewhat more restricted topic than the migration of population. We shall not consider children who move with their parents or people who move at or after retirement. The migration of the retired and the migration of active workers are governed by quite different considerations. The retired often seek more pleasant climates and low living costs that will augment the real value of their pensions and social security benefits. They may frequently return to their place of origin, which they left earlier to pursue their careers.

The propensity of workers to migrate toward places where incomes are higher is immediately apparent where there are gross disparities in income levels. The tremendous flow of immigrants to the United States from Southern and Eastern Europe before World War I is a conspicuous example, as are the flows from Puerto Rico to the mainland United States and from the West Indies, Pakistan, and India to Great Britain after World War II. Many such migration flows would have been far larger or would have continued much longer had they not been restricted by rigid control of immigration by the receiving countries. The flows after World War II illustrate also the role of costs; in many of these cases a prewar trickle became a large postwar stream when air transport became available at fares far below those of passenger ships. Yet it would be incorrect to give the impression that only economic forces govern the international migration of labor. Many migrants are refugees from war or from political, religious, or racial persecution. Sometimes refugees blaze a path that is then followed by others whose motives are more largely economic.

Most countries regard the outflow of unskilled labor tolerantly, and most restrict its inflow. But attitudes become quite different toward international flows of highly skilled labor such as scientists, engineers, and physicians. The concern of the countries of origin is expressed in the common term *brain drain*, while many receiving countries give preference to immigrants with scarce skills. The professional worker who changes countries usually gets higher income and, frequently, better working facilities and opportunities for advancement. But his home country, which seldom views the permanent emigrant as part of the group whose welfare it seeks to maximize, is concerned that it has invested in his education and does not share the returns.[4]

In view of the large volume of international migration that takes place despite great barriers of cost and legal restrictions, it sometimes seems surprising that there is not more internal migration than there is. Of course, income disparities between regions within countries are usually much smaller than those between developed and less-developed countries, but some are nevertheless substantial. Why do not more people move from Mississippi to Chicago or from South Carolina to New York? More specifically, when there is freedom of movement, why is there not enough migration to wipe out the income differential that gives rise to it? To deal with these questions we need a model of the decision to migrate.

The analysis of returns to migration is very similar to the analysis of returns to education in Chapter 3 and can be illustrated by referring back to Figure 3. Income stream *A* can now be interpreted as the expected income if the worker migrates, and income stream *B* as the expected income stream if he does not. The area marked 1 represents the out-of-pocket costs of migration, such as fares and the costs of moving belongings, and area 2 represents income lost in job search after migration. This area disappears in cases where the worker is unemployed at the time he decides to move. The period of costs should be compressed into a shorter time than it occupies in Figure 3, and the out-of-pocket costs may be incurred before the search costs rather than simultaneously with them. If we discount the costs and returns back to the time when the worker is deciding whether to move, we can calculate an internal rate of return on migration or the present value of moving at a given interest rate.

In a formal sense, this exercise solves the problem. The workers who move are those who expect an internal rate of return higher than their own rate of time preference, or subjective discount rate, or for whom the present value of moving is positive. However, this still leaves formidable difficulties, particularly in estimating the income streams. If we performed this calculation using average incomes of factory workers in Illinois and Mississippi, identifiable moving costs such as rail coach fares, and a modest initial period of unemployment after migration—say two months—we would calculate an extremely high return.[5] Is such a high return plausible? Perhaps so. If the initial investment takes more resources than most Mississippi workers can command, then they cannot make it no matter how high the returns. And those who can move only by risking almost all of their small capital will demand rates of return that are very high by the standards of large investors. The short time horizon of low-income families and the high rate at which they discount the future are demonstrated by the high interest rates they are willing to pay to buy on credit.[6] Nevertheless, the example overstates the return to migration in several ways. First, it will not do to calculate the returns using the incomes of all people in the two areas. At a minimum, we must control for education and race, since the average number of years of school completed is lower in Mississippi than in Illinois and the percentage of blacks is higher—and migration does not change one's color or increase one's schooling.

Even this correction is too small. Since migration probably selects those with greater-than-average ability and initiative, the migrant might have fared better than the average of those of his race and education had he stayed at home. Moreover, he cannot be sure of doing as well in the destination area as otherwise-similar nonmigrants do. Employers give preference to local workers whose references are easily checked and who are less likely to quit because of homesickness or family emergencies that call them back to the South. Even after an initial period of unemployment has ended, the migrant may be more exposed to the possibility of future unemployment than the nonmigrant. And he may have to accept lower wages because he does not yet have some of the specialized skills that explain part of the high average earnings in the new area.

The unemployment rate of migrants not only is higher than that of nonmigrants, but it varies more with changes in business conditions. A small reduction in demand could cause only a slight increase in the unemployment of established workers yet cause a great reduction in new hires. For this reason the accession rate may be a better measure of the migrant's chances of finding work than the unemployment rate. The sensitivity of rates of migration to business conditions in the destination areas is sometimes quite startling.[7] Even where the risk of unemployment is in fact reasonably small, it may be exaggerated in the mind of the potential migrant.

Our example of a way of estimating a return to migration used streams of money income in the two areas. In principle, these streams should be adjusted for differences in the prices of consumer goods. Unfortunately, no such cross-sectional price indexes exist; but if they did, they would undoubtedly correlate positively with money income, making the geographic differences in real income smaller than those in nominal income.[8]

The difficulties of estimation are no less when one turns from incomes to costs. These must include the psychic costs of leaving families, friends, and familiar surroundings for a strange and hostile environment. The psychic costs of breaking ties with the home community no doubt increase with age faster than the money costs of moving people and possessions.

To be sure, migrants have ways of reducing psychic costs, of which the most obvious is to congregate in particular neighborhoods in the destination cities and to establish stores, bars, clubs, and churches that reflect their special tastes. To some extent such concentration in slum neighborhoods is enforced by poverty and racial discrimination, but it goes beyond what can be explained on these grounds. It is true of white migrants from South to North as well as of black, so much so that particular blocks in Chicago and Detroit may be almost entirely occupied by white migrants from one Tennessee or Kentucky county.

Yet despite the efforts to replicate home institutions in the destination area, many migrants return home, disappointed with life in their new location. The probability that migration will end in a reverse move also lowers the a priori return. Even for those who remain in the new area, the costs of transportation are more than the cost of the first trip. The cost of later visits home at times of illness or death in the family or for holidays must also be counted. Such costs help to explain why the power of income differentials to induce migration is sharply diminished by increases in distance between origin and destination.[9] If the distance is so great that the cost of visits home is prohibitive, this must be counted among the psychic costs of migration.

Difficult as it is for economists to estimate the return on migration, it is even more difficult for the prospective migrant. He has few sources of information about labor-market conditions in different possible destination areas, and even after he has moved he will usually be badly informed about how to find a job in the new market. The principal source of information is letters and visits from friends and relatives who have moved earlier. Recruiting at long distance by employers is largely restricted to managerial and professional occupations, as is the use of interarea clearance of job vacancies in the public employment service. Improvements in data processing may increase the role of the employment service in assisting geographical mobility, though it is hard to devise a substitute for being met by an old friend when one arrives in a strange city.

We have so far defined the income streams of migrants and those who remain behind in terms of earned income. This may be too narrow a view. Other kinds of income also are higher in the destination areas, especially unemployment-insurance benefits and welfare payments. While migrants may at first not qualify for such benefits, eventually they will.[10] This should not be interpreted as meaning that people migrate in order to get on welfare. Rather, the existence of a more generous welfare and unemployment-insurance system in the destination area reduces the risks of migration and, specifically, reduces the cost to be attached to the probability of unemployment after the initial period of getting established.

THE EFFECTS OF MIGRATION
ON WAGE DIFFERENTIALS

Economic theory has long predicted that income differentials between areas would induce migration flows, and all of the evidence suggests that they do. But the theory goes on to predict that the migration of labor, together with the reverse migration of capital, will bring the incomes of different areas into equality (within a country or region of free migration and capital movement), and this they have not yet done. The disparity arises because the traditional theory is designed to deal with a system in equilibrium that is disturbed by a single shock. For example, the discovery of valuable minerals in a sparsely settled region would create a shortage of labor, which would raise wages substantially and induce migration. When the new industry and any secondary industries that it generated were fully established and staffed, no further migration would be needed. As wages rose elsewhere, wages in the mining region would fail to keep pace; eventually the differential in its favor would disappear.

Most disequilibria are not caused by single events, however. Employment growth is greater year after year in the major urban industrial areas than in rural areas heavily dependent on agriculture, mining, forestry, or fishing. At the same time, the natural rate of population increase may be higher in declining rural areas than in the urban centers, and the level of educational attainment in rural areas is lower.

In the case of a one-time disturbance, any positive rate of net migration in the direction of the area with higher income would eventually close the income gap. But the dynamic disturbance caused by a growth rate of population of working age that exceeds the growth rate of employment can be alleviated only by a rate of migration larger than the difference between the two growth rates. Despite heavy out-migration, some areas can therefore have continuing surpluses of unskilled labor. Like the Red Queen, they must run very fast just to stay in the same place.

The conditions under which migration will equalize incomes in different regions are more stringent than those needed to create an upward-sloping supply curve of labor for each region, measured with wages relative to other regions on the vertical axis. A high relative wage will induce migration of labor and augment the region's labor supply. A low relative wage will induce more young people reaching working age to move away and seek employment elsewhere. The out-migration of the young from a declining area will leave an older work force with a high rate of retirement, while the growing area will have a younger, more flexible work force. Unfortunately, these characteristics of the work force are likely to inhibit the movement of industry into areas of labor surplus, though such movement should be the complement of the outflow of labor.

The declining area may have excess capacity in its schools, hospitals, and other public facilities, while facilities in the growing areas become increasingly congested. Governments often attempt to prevent such imbalances by some degree of subsidy to encourage the location of industry in areas of labor surplus. To the extent that solving all problems of regional imbalance by the migration of labor involves wastes in social overhead capital, the subsidy of alternative solutions makes good sense.

NOTES

1. For a more complete account of this process, see Charles C. Holt and Martin H. David, "The Concept of Job Vacancies in a Dynamic Theory of the Labor Market," in *The Measurement and Interpretation of Job Vacancies* (New York: National Bureau of Economic Research, 1966) .

2. This hypothesis that the employer can substitute search costs for wages was first advanced by George J. Stigler in "Information in the Labor Market," *Journal of Political Economy* **70** (October 1962, Supplement) , 94–105. For some empirical results that tend to confirm the hypothesis, see A. Rees and G. P. Shultz, *Workers and Wages in an Urban Labor Market* (Chicago: University of Chicago Press, 1970) , pp. 207–210.

3. See George P. Shultz and Arnold E. Weber, *Strategies for the Displaced Worker* (New York: Harper & Row, 1966) .

4. If there is only marginal migration and the migrant has been receiving his marginal product, there is no loss to those left behind. But this conclusion does not necessarily hold for flows that are larger than marginal. For a careful analysis of this issue, see R. A. Berry and R. Soligo, "Some Welfare Aspects of International Migration," *Journal of Political Economy* **77** (September 1969) , 778–794.

5. In July 1970, average weekly wages in manufacturing in Illinois were $50 a week above those in Mississippi. For a worker who could expect to be employed continuously at the average manufacturing job in either state, this would amount to about $2,500 a year. A worker considering moving at age 25 and retiring at 65 would in principle want to know the present value of an annuity of $2,500 for 40 years. At an interest rate of 8 percent, this comes to roughly $30,000, clearly far in excess of the costs of transporting a worker, his family, and his possessions, and the loss of two months' wages during and after the move.

6. See David Caplovitz, *The Poor Pay More* (New York: Free Press, 1963) .

7. For example, from 1907 to 1908 the estimated unemployment rate in the United States rose from 1.8 percent to 8.5 percent. The number of immigrants declined from 1,285,000 to 783,000. See U.S. Bureau of Census, *Historical Statistics of the United States,* Series D-47 and C-88.

8. The city workers' family budgets of the U.S. Bureau of Labor Statistics reflect

differences in the composition of consumption and standard of living between cities, as well as differences in price levels.

9. See Larry A. Sjaastad, "Income and Migration in the United States," unpublished doctoral dissertation, University of Chicago, 1961.

10. In New York City in 1967, 32 percent of the mothers in households receiving Aid to Families of Dependent Children were born in Latin America (largely in Puerto Rico). This figure is taken from an unpublished paper by Daniel Saks.

CHAPTER 7

Unemployment
and Unfilled Vacancies

Unemployment can be divided into two basic types: unemployment that results from deficient aggregate demand, and all other unemployment. The latter in turn is often divided into frictional, structural, and seasonal unemployment.

We have seen in the last chapter that unemployment and unfilled vacancies exist simultaneously because it takes time to match jobs and men appropriately. The unemployment that accompanies this matching process is *frictional unemployment*, which, strictly defined, is unemployment that corresponds to unfilled vacancies in the same occupations and the same places. More stubborn frictions result when the unemployed are mismatched with job vacancies because they do not have the right skills or live in the wrong places. Such mismatching creates *structural unemployment*, a concept that will be examined in more detail below. Finding

112

jobs for the structurally unemployed requires more than search in local markets; workers must be retrained, or jobs or workers must move to new locations. The term *seasonal unemployment* is self-explanatory. Seasonal unemployment occurs in such activities as construction, agriculture, canning, and the tourist trade, in which weather or the calendar determine when production can be carried on or govern the level of demand. For purposes of measuring the business cycle and the strength of demand in the labor market, it is usual to use unemployment statistics that have been seasonally adjusted. This adjustment does not remove the seasonal component of unemployment from the total; it merely spreads it evenly over the year.

In contrast with all of these, we provisionally define *demand-deficiency unemployment* as unemployment that occurs when there is not enough aggregate demand to provide work for the whole labor force no matter how it is trained or deployed. This implies that in the economy as a whole there are more unemployed workers than vacant jobs. An older term for this condition is *cyclical unemployment*. The more awkward term *demand-deficiency unemployment* has the virtue of indicating that there may not be adequate demand even at a business cycle peak, as in 1937.

A second way of classifying unemployment is to divide it into voluntary and involuntary unemployment. The basic idea of the division is that a worker is voluntarily unemployed when he has been offered a job that he could fill but continues to search for a better job at a higher wage rather than accept the offer. The extent to which he will continue to search rather than accept one of the first offers he gets is determined by two sets of factors. The first is his resources as measured by savings, ability to borrow, unemployment-insurance benefits, and support from family or friends. The second is his expectations about the state of the labor market and his ideas, which may be quite firm, about the kind of job it is appropriate for him to take. A worker is involuntarily unemployed if he would be willing to accept a job for which he is qualified at the prevailing wage or below it, but cannot find any such job. Thus voluntary unemployment is essentially frictional, while involuntary unemployment is demand-deficiency unemployment.

These definitions conceal a number of serious problems. Even when there is heavy unemployment, some unpleasant, low-wage jobs may remain unfilled because no one wants them. If a skilled worker loses a high-wage job and turns down a low-wage job while searching for work at his old trade, is he voluntarily or involuntarily unemployed, or both at once? Some writers say that he is voluntarily unemployed and that therefore all unemployment even in depressions is voluntary.[1] But this view involves an aggregation fallacy. If the job is very unpleasant and badly paid, 100 men might turn it down. Yet if any one of them took it, the vacancy open to the other 99 would disappear. The common view therefore relates involuntary unemployment to the numerical balance between vacancies and unemployed men, which is the subject of the following section.

THE RELATION BETWEEN UNEMPLOYMENT AND VACANCIES

The general form of the relationship between total vacancies and total unemployment is shown in Figure 12, where vacancies are measured on the vertical axis and unemployment is measured on the horizontal axis.[2] For any given structure of the labor market,

FIGURE 12
The Relationship Between Unemployment and Job Vacancies

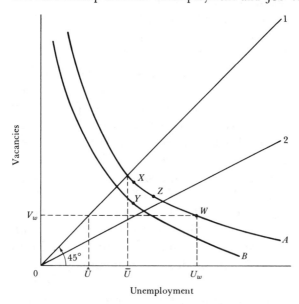

vacancies and unemployment are negatively related along a curve such as the one marked *A*. These curves are drawn convex to the origin for reasons that will become apparent shortly. At very low levels of unemployment the number of unfilled vacancies can rise quite rapidly with little effect in reducing frictional unemployment. Although the average duration of unemployment declines as good jobs become easy to find, a tight labor market also encourages some workers to quit their jobs in search of better ones, and this limits the fall in the unemployment rate. Similarly, even at very high unemployment rates there are some unfilled vacancies for workers with very special qualifications or in the least attractive jobs. These openings determine some positive minimum level of vacancies for any market structure. Thus the curve cannot touch either axis and must therefore be convex.[3]

Improvement of the functioning of the labor market, or reductions in structural unemployment achieved by retraining or the relocation of workers or jobs, will shift the relation between unemployment and vacancies toward the origin, producing a new curve such as *B*. Along this curve there are fewer vacancies and less unemployment for any given level of aggregate demand. Increases in aggregate demand result in movements to the left along the curve representing a given market structure; decreases in aggregate demand produce movements to the right along such a curve.

All positions at which the number of unemployed workers is equal to the number of vacancies lie on the 45-degree ray from the origin, marked 1. This ray forms one common basis for distinguishing between full and less-than-full employment. To the right of this ray there is said to be demand deficiency, because the number of unemployed exceeds the number of vacancies; to the left there is not. This implies that there is more than one possible position of full employment; indeed, there is a different one for each possible structure of the labor market.

Although the 45-degree line indicates a quantitative balance between the demand for labor and the supply, it does not necessarily indicate equilibrium in the average level of wages. It is clear that to the left of this line wages must tend to rise as employers improve their wage offers in an effort to fill vacancies. But where the labor market is made up of different submarkets or sectors, this may also be true for some distance to the right of the 45-degree line. The sectors may consist of different occupations or different geographical locations.

Let us assume that money wages are rigid downward in each sector and that wages will rise in any sector in which there are more vacancies than unemployed workers. The average level of wages will then rise as long as there is excess demand in any sector. The positions in which there is no excess demand in any market must lie to the right of those in which there is no excess demand in the aggregate, perhaps along a ray such as that marked 2. The average level of money wages would then be stable to the right of ray 2 and rising, perhaps at increasing rates, as one moves to the left of this ray.

Where there are no comprehensive statistics on unfilled vacancies, as in the United States, it is especially hard to distinguish increases in unemployment resulting from a decline in aggregate demand from increases resulting from greater structural imbalance. Where vacancy statistics are available, the former would be indicated by a movement such as that from X to Z, with vacancies decreasing as unemployment increased. The latter would be indicated by a movement such as that from Y to Z. In the absence of vacancy statistics, the second type of movement might be identified by the increasing dispersion of geographical and occupational unemployment rates, since growing structural imbalance would involve constant or falling unemployment in sectors where the number of vacancies was increasing, and rising unemployment in other sectors.

An increase in unemployment with no change in vacancies—a horizontal shift to the right from an initial position on Figure 12—represents a simultaneous increase in structural and demand-deficiency unemployment.

Figure 12 can be used to explore ways in which a given total of unemployment can be broken down into two components, one of which represents demand deficiency and the other frictional and structural unemployment. Suppose that we are at point W on curve A, with unemployment of U_w and vacancies of V_w. If we accept the definition that there is no demand deficiency when the total number of vacancies equals the total number of unemployed, then a first approximation is to substract V_w from U_w and call the difference demand-deficiency unemployment. This would put the boundary between the components at $\hat{U}$, with the distance $O\hat{U}$ equal to the frictional and structural component. However, it is clear from the diagram that the distance $\hat{U}U_w$ overstates the number of jobs that needs to be created by increasing demand. If demand is increased with no change in the market structure, the point describing the state of the market will move leftward along A, and equality between unemployment and vacancies will be reached at the unemployment level $\bar{U}$, on ray 1. At this point the frictional and structural component, $O\bar{U}$, is larger than $O\hat{U}$. The increased demand for labor has not consisted entirely of demand for people with the skills and in the locations represented by the unemployed, and the number of unfilled vacancies has therefore risen.

An alternative concept of demand deficiency, which produces a much smaller estimate of demand-deficiency unemployment, states that there is insufficient aggregate demand only if unemployment is greater than the amount consistent with a stable price level.[4] The boundaries suggested by this definition would lie to the right of their analogues $\hat{U}$ and $\bar{U}$, but not so far to the right as to make the role of ray 2 analogous to that of ray 1. Ray 2 represents stable average wages, and price stability would involve less unemployment than this because the growth of average productivity (output per man-hour) permits rising average money wages to be consistent with stable prices.

Figure 12 does not provide any basis for distinguishing between frictional and structural unemployment. It should be noted, however, that if frictional unemployment is defined as unemployment matched by vacancies in the same market, then the boundary between frictional and structural unemployment depends on how markets are defined. The greater the number of different occupations and localities considered as separate markets, the smaller the frictional component of unemployment and the larger the structural component.

THE STRUCTURE
OF UNEMPLOYMENT

Unemployment rates at any time have a pronounced structure by place, industry, occupation, and type of worker—a structure that does not change greatly over the business cycle. This structure can be related to a number of factors already considered. Selected unemployment rates for 1971 are shown in Tables 10 and 11. These rates are the percentage of the civilian labor force unemployed in each group. The structure of rates shown is broadly similar to that of other recent years.

A number of features of these tables are consistent with the theory of fixed costs of employment, which predicts lower unemployment where the investment in the employee is greatest. Unemployment rates are generally higher for women than for men at ages beyond 24, which is probably a result of the less-continuous participation in the labor force by women and their need to search for new jobs when they reenter the labor market. Unemployment rates are substantially lower in the occupations that require high levels of skill and education. This reflects the greater stability of employment created by higher fixed costs. It may also indicate that those skilled workers who do become unemployed usually have an easier time finding new jobs. This second effect is independent of the fixed-cost hypothesis. It suggests that there has been a faster growth in the number of skilled and educated workers demanded than in the number available; the rapid growth of the demand is related to the nature of recent technological change, which has tended to displace unskilled and semiskilled workers and to require more skilled and professional workers. The

TABLE 10

Unemployment Rates by Age, Sex, and Color, 1971

Age	Males		Females	
	White	Negro and Other	White	Negro and Other
16 and 17	17.1	33.4	16.7	38.5
18 and 19	13.5	26.0	14.1	33.7
20–24	9.4	16.2	8.5	17.3
25–34	4.0	7.4	6.3	10.7
35–44	2.9	4.9	4.9	6.9
45–54	2.8	4.5	3.9	4.2
55–64	3.2	4.7	3.3	3.5
65 and over	3.4	3.4	3.6	3.9
Total, 16 and over	4.9	9.1	6.3	10.8

Source: *Manpower Report of the President*, **March 1972**, Table A-16.

longer-term tendencies in this direction were reversed in the recession of 1970–1971, when unusually high unemployment was experienced by such groups as scientists and engineers. This was related to a decline in government expenditure on scientific research and development.

The high rate of unemployment of teenage workers also is consistent with the fixed-cost hypothesis. Young workers have little specific training and are usually employed in relatively unskilled jobs, where they can be among the first dismissed if demand decreases. Many move in and out of the labor force frequently, because they are in school most of the year and must search for a new job at the time of each entry. Even those teenagers who have left school are trying out different jobs to see what kind of work they want to do; they often quit jobs that do not turn out to be agreeable and must then look for new ones. The costs of such shopping-around are not very high for those who still live with their families, and the experience gained may often be valuable in the choice of a more congenial eventual career.

The high teenage unemployment rate of the United States is not found in most European countries. In part this is a result of the generally tighter labor markets in Europe, but more specific factors are also at work. Labor-market institutions in Europe may

---

TABLE 11

Unemployment Rates by Occupation Group, 1971

White-collar workers	3.5	
Professional and technical workers		2.9
Managers, proprietors, and officials		1.6
Clerical workers		4.8
Sales workers		4.3
Blue-collar workers	7.4	
Craftsmen and foremen		4.7
Operatives		8.3
Nonfarm laborers		10.8
Service workers	6.3	
Private household workers		4.5
Other service workers		6.6
Farmers and farm laborers	2.6	

Source: *Manpower Report of the President,* March 1972, Table A-17.

be better designed to facilitate the transition from school to work by providing school-leavers with vocational training and information about the labor market. Some countries (Great Britain, for example) have an explicit system of youth or juvenile wage rates, which start substantially below the adult rate and rise with each year of age. This makes the teenager a "good buy" for employers in jobs that can be learned quickly. In the United States juveniles usually receive the same rates as adults for a given job, except perhaps for a few months at a lower trainee or probationary rate.

The unemployment rate in 1971 for married men with spouse present was 3.2 percent, which is far below the average for all men. This is the counterpart of the higher labor-force-participation rate of married men discussed in Chapter 1. Again the chain of causation may be complex. Disadvantages or disabilities that cause men to remain bachelors or that make their marriages unstable could also make it harder for them to find jobs. The greater financial pressures on married men could induce them to engage in more intensive job search and to end it more quickly by accepting the best opening discovered. Where this financial pressure is severe, the married man's investment in job search could be less than optimal. A married man is also less likely to quit a job than a single man, and employers prefer married men on this account.

The 1971 ratio of nonwhite to white unemployment rates was slightly below two; this ratio has been in the neighborhood of two since the mid-1950s and has not yet been brought down appreciably by government policies designed to eliminate racial discrimination in employment. To some extent the unemployment rates reflect racial differences in educational attainment and in occupation. More than 90 percent of nonwhites are blacks, who are concentrated in the least-skilled occupations and on average have somewhat fewer years of schooling than whites. Blacks are disproportionately represented in such occupations as laborers, domestic servants, and service workers, where much employment is casual and there is little on-the-job training. However, substantial differences in unemployment rates by color are also present within occupations.[5] These differences reflect direct discrimination in the hiring process rather than the indirect effects of discrimination in other forms. Racial discrimination in labor markets will be discussed at greater length in Chapter 12.

The high rate of unemployment of black workers does not mean that there are no job vacancies for blacks; there may be vacancies, but only for low-wage work with unpleasant working conditions and no prospect of advancement. These vacancies are often turned down in the hope of finding something better, or the jobs are taken only to be left quickly if they prove to be too disagreeable.[6]

In addition to the unemployment differentials shown in Tables 10 and 11, there are important differentials in unemployment rates by geographical area. Some of these are temporary and reflect the effects of the business cycle. A recession produces substantial lay-offs among workers in the durable-goods industries, since purchases of durable goods are easily postponed in bad times. This leads to geographical concentrations of unemployment in the centers of durable-goods production. Workers with seniority in such high-wage industries as steel or automobiles are unlikely to move in search of work during a recession. Since they expect to be recalled to a good job, their best course is to wait the recession out, supported by unemployment insurance, dissaving, and supplementary unemployment benefits in the industries where it is provided. A few of these unemployed workers will find occasional work outside their usual industry, but where the whole area is depressed, such opportunities are infrequent.

Other geographic concentrations of unemployment are long lived, reflecting the decline of localized industries or the large-scale displacement of labor by technological change. In the 1950s such geographic concentrations of unemployment were produced by the decline of the New England textile industry and by the replacement of steam locomotives with diesels. Since the diesel engine requires far less maintenance than a steam engine, employment in railroad repair shops declined, and these were the main employers in a number of small towns. In the 1960s similar pockets of unemployment have been caused by the closing of obsolete meat-packing plants and, on a larger scale, by declining employment in coal mining. The drop in employment caused by increasing mechanization of coal mining in the face of rather static demand has tended to make the entire Appalachian area a depressed area.

In the larger depressed communities the combination of unemployed labor and vacant factories often attracts new industry. The growth of employment in plastics, electronics, and other light industries has helped reduce to reasonable levels the unemployment rates in some of the old New England textile towns. In contrast, many of the former mining and railroad towns are too far from markets and materials to be attractive locations for new establishments. Here labor bears the brunt of the adjustment; many younger workers migrate, and older ones may simply drop out of the labor force.

NOTES

1. See, for example, R. E. Lucas and L. J. Rapping, "Real Wages, Employment and Inflation," *Journal of Political Economy* (September–October 1969), 721–754.
2. The general form of this diagram follows J. C. R. Dow and L. A. Dicks-Mireaux, "The Excess Demand for Labor, A Study of Conditions in Great Britain, 1946–1956," *Oxford Economic Papers* (February 1958), 1–33.
3. Where changes in the unemployment rate are within a narrow range, the non-linearity of the relation may not be apparent. For Great Britain for 1949–1966, A. P. Thirlwall has estimated the relation to be linear:

$$U = 2.989 - 0.908V, r^2 = 0.682,$$
$$(0.223) \quad (0.150)$$

when U is the unemployment rate, V is the vacancy rate, and the figures in parentheses are standard errors. See "Types of Unemployment with Special Reference to 'Non-Demand Deficient' Unemployment in Great Britain," *Scottish Journal of Political Economy* 16 (February 1969), 20–49. Similar estimates cannot be made for the United States, where vacancy statistics have not been collected regularly until very recently.
4. A variant of this definition advanced by Lipsey would say that there is insufficient aggregate demand when unemployment is more than enough to keep the rise in prices below that regarded as acceptable by policy makers. This is useful for the policy makers themselves, but not to others because of its complete subjectivity. See R. G. Lipsey, "Structural and Demand Deficient Unemployment Reconsidered," in A. M. Ross, ed., *Employment Policy and the Labor Market* (Berkeley: University of California Press, 1965).
5. See Harry J. Gilman, "Economic Discrimination and Unemployment," *American Economic Review* 55 (1965), 1077–1096.
6. See Elliott Liebow, *Talley's Corner: A Study of Negro Street-Corner Men* (Boston: Little, Brown, 1968), chap. 2; and Peter B. Doeringer, "Manpower Programs for Ghetto Labor Markets," Industrial Relations Research Association, *Proceedings of the Twenty-First Annual Winter Meetings* (1969).

PART IV

Economic Aspects of Trade Unions

Union Goals

FORMAL MODELS OF UNION OBJECTIVES

So far our discussion of labor markets has considered the behavior of individual workers and employers, with only passing reference to trade unions. Clearly this neglect must be remedied, for unions and collective bargaining now play a central role in the determination of wage levels and wage structures, as well as in many other aspects of the employment relation. About 30 percent of nonagricultural employees have been union members in recent years, and the effects of collective bargaining extend beyond the limits of its coverage.

Our discussion will focus on the economic functions of the trade union to the exclusion of its role as a social and political institution. Even within the area of collective bargaining, nothing will be said about such topics as grievance machinery and seniority.

125

The omitted areas are extremely important, of course, but the kind of analysis useful in dealing with them is very different from the somewhat formal economic analysis used here.

What is left to consider is the role of unions in determining wages and the level of employment. A union's concern with the total amount of employment is part of its broader concern with job scarcity and job security. The term *job security* includes the union's concern for the distribution of employment among members and for the job tenure of the individual members. In formal models, however, the focus is limited to the less-inclusive goals of increasing total employment and expanding union membership; thus the models represent what may be an excessively narrow view of the union's concern with employment. But even in the narrowed field remaining, the formal models are not always successful.

In discussing the demand for labor in Part II, we used as a starting point the model of the profit-maximizing firm. This model must sometimes be modified, especially for large firms whose policies are directed by managers rather than by owners. Nevertheless, the value of the concept of profit maximization as a point of departure for analysis is very great.

It is much more difficult, if not impossible, to analyze union behavior by constructing a simple model of a trade union as a maximizer of anything, which implies a single goal common to the entire organization. Far more than the firm, the union is both an economic and a political entity. Though ultimate power nominally rests with stockholders in the corporation and with members in the union, both corporate management and union leadership play critical roles in determining policy. But in many unions wage bargains must be taken back to the membership for ratification, and leadership decisions are not always routinely endorsed. As a tactic in negotiation with management, leaders may sometimes send agreements back for ratification knowing that they are unacceptable; at other times they are genuinely surprised by the repudiation of a bargain they firmly believed to be the best obtainable. In contrast, corporate management and directors have full authority to negotiate wages without consulting the stockholders. In the long run they may suffer if they make a bad bargain, but in the short run their decisions will not be challenged.

Furthermore, the union leader faces greater risks than the corporate director when he seeks reelection. In corporations the rule of one share-one vote makes it very expensive to challenge management by soliciting proxies where management controls large blocks of stock. In contrast, the one man, one vote rule of unions, though it does not eliminate the advantages of incumbents, poses greater potential threats. In recent years three major American national unions have had their presidents replaced in contested elections in which the incumbent lost: the United Steelworkers; the International Union of Electrical Workers; and the State, County, and Municipal Workers.

The sharing of power in the union between leadership and membership creates difficulties in constructing a formal model of union behavior because there may be differences in aims or emphasis between leaders and the rank and file. The leader wants to head a large and stable organization and to expand its membership; he may become interested in extending his personal influence in the larger labor movement or on the national political scene. The members, on the other hand, are interested primarily in job security, higher wages, and good working conditions. And union leaders pursue these goals as well as their personal goals—both because they believe in them and because their own jobs may be threatened if they do not.

A second source of difficulty in constructing a formal model of union behavior is that the gains won by unions in collective bargaining do not go to the organization as such but to the individual members directly, and there is no mechanism for the secondary redistribution of these gains. This is in sharp contrast with the corporation, where profits go to the firm before there is any distribution to stockholders. Some profits—often a major part of the total—are not distributed at all, and profits made in one establishment or activity within the corporation can be used in expanding another.

Keeping these difficulties in mind, we can now consider possible formal models of union wage policy. It is sometimes suggested that a union should behave like a product-market monopolist. Figure 13 illustrates such behavior. The curve D is the downward-sloping demand curve for union labor. Where all the firms producing for a given market are organized, the demand curve for union labor

FIGURE 13
Two Maximizing Models of Union Wage Goals

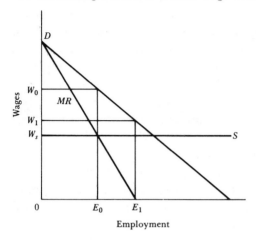

is determined by the factors that were considered in Part II. Where some of the firms in a product market are not organized, an increase in wages in the organized sector will enlarge the share of the nonunion firms in total sales of the product, and this indirect substitution of nonunion for union labor will make the demand for union labor more elastic than in the case of complete organization. The line labelled S is a horizontal supply curve of union labor to one firm, and MR is the *marginal revenue* curve corresponding to D, which shows the addition to the total wage bill produced by lowering the wage just enough to permit the employment of one more man.[1] Following the analogue of the product-market monopolist, the union would seek to set the wage W_0, at which marginal revenue is equal to the supply price of labor. For a product-market monopolist, the analogous price would maximize profit. But for the union, this particular equality has no meaning. Wage W_0 is above the supply price of labor and is therefore more than is needed to get another union member to accept employment. But, as compared to the slightly higher wage at which one more member would remain unemployed, it involves a small loss in wages to each member already employed. Since the wage loss and the employment gain do not accrue to the same people, it is of no use to treat wages in excess of the supply price as a fund to be maximized. The union leader must balance the pressures (by employed members) for higher wages against the pressures (by unemployed members) for work, keeping in mind the political importance of each group within the union—and this balancing will not lead to the maximization solution, except by mere chance.

The rule sometimes suggested that unions should try to maximize the wage bill is even worse. This would involve setting employment at E_1 where MR is zero; if the demand for union labor is elastic at the nonunion wage, the corresponding wage, W_1, will be below the wage W_s that would prevail with no union. It is impossible to see why any union membership or honest union leadership would want such a solution. Nor would the employer want it, since he would be unable to recruit labor.

The difficulties of a maximization model can be illustrated more clearly by considering the case of an industrial union that includes two distinct classes of members—a small group of craftsmen and a large group of operatives. We assume that the demand for craftsmen is very inelastic and that the demand for operatives is quite elastic. The product-market analogue is the case of the discriminating monopolist selling the same product in two separate markets. Here the solution that maximizes profit is to have marginal revenue in each market equal to the common marginal cost or supply price, which implies a higher price in the market where demand is less elastic. But if the union makes large wage gains for its craft members and small ones or none for the more numerous operatives, it has no way to channel part of the craft gains to the others. Such a policy will therefore put the union leaders in severe political trouble. They are forced to settle for a smaller total gain more equitably distributed, and there is good evidence that for this reason the craft members of industrial unions sometimes fare badly.[2]

A more promising way to look at the formation of union wage goals is to regard them as influenced by at least two separate elements: the size of union membership and the wage level. The goals in question here are those for which the union is prepared to strike if necessary, as distinguished from initial bargaining demands, which may far exceed what the union expects to get. The relative weights to be attached to membership and wages will vary from union to union, with more weight given to the size of the membership in industrial unions than is given in craft unions, and more weight given to size of membership in unions that are interested in social and political reform than is given in so-called business unions interested largely in advancing the position of their own present members.

If we had chosen wages and employment, rather than wages and membership, as the two principal elements in the formation of union goals, we could have assumed from the downward slope of the demand curve for union labor that they were negatively related, and we could then have drawn a preference function like an indifference curve expressing the rate at which the union is willing to trade one of these goals for the other.[3] However, when a union has not organized its entire potential jurisdiction, the potential gains in membership from a policy of high wages, which is helpful in extending organization, could in some cases more than offset the contraction of employment among present members. In such a case the national leadership of the union (though not necessarily the local leadership) would prefer the high-wage strategy on both counts.

An interesting example of different choices made by two national unions facing apparently similar circumstances is afforded by events in the meat-packing industry in the early 1960s. Some major firms in the industry threatened to close a number of unprofitable unionized plants unless the unions agreed to wage reductions. The local unions concerned reacted differently to these threats, depending on local labor market conditions. However, the Amalgamated Meat Cutters and Butcher Workmen influenced its local unions to accept wage reductions, because it had organized many small plants, especially in the South, that faced competition from low-wage, nonunion firms. It felt that it could grow only through a wage policy of moderation. In contrast, the United Packinghouse Workers influenced its locals to refuse the wage cuts and to accept the plant shutdowns. It was interested in organizing large new independent packing companies in the Midwest and felt that it could best do so by a policy of militance.[4] If the case of the United Packinghouse Workers were analyzed as a choice between wages and employment, it would appear that employment had no weight in the union's preference function. When employment is replaced by membership as the second element of the preference function, both elements play a role.

FACTORS INFLUENCING
WAGE POLICY

One important feature of union wage policy is the critical role of the current money wage. A union will almost always insist on maintaining the current wage even at the cost of severe contraction in employment, whereas it would not insist on increasing the money wage if the consequences for employment were anything like as severe. In other words, the weight given to the size of membership or employment is much smaller for wage cuts than for wage increases. This downward rigidity of the money wage now extends to nonunion portions of the economy as well, perhaps in part because nonunion employers have feared that wage reductions would encourage unionization. There have been no general reductions in money wages in any important industry since the early 1930s, though there have been several moderately severe recessions and a number of major industries have had declining employment.

Unions have occasionally agreed to wage reductions at the firm or establishment level when there has been a threat that an establishment would shut down or be relocated and the promise that a wage reduction would avert this. Such a position will seem credible only when taken by a management with whom the union has had good relations. Even in such cases, the union can agree only if the concession to one firm does not provide an occasion for other unionzed employers to demand similar treatment. For this reason, a union cannot make wage concessions to one employer in a group engaged in multiemployer bargaining. However, it can try to help one employer improve productivity, which is a much less-visible kind of concession.

As Keynes pointed out in the *General Theory*, union resistance to cuts in real wages that arise from increases in the level of consumer prices is much less rapid and less complete than resistance to cuts in money wages. A money-wage cut initiated or proposed by an employer is a direct affront, because it always involves cutting wages relative to wages elsewhere. In contrast, a fall in real wages produced by an increase in the price level is impersonal, because it affects everyone. Moreover, it is not immediately perceived. This does not mean that unions or their members are so much the victims of money illusion that they will not respond to prolonged or severe rises in consumer prices. Once they have passed some threshold, such price rises will strengthen union demands for wage increases and may also assist unions in organizing new industries and areas.[5]

The wage demands of any one union are strongly influenced by comparisons with other groups of workers with whom there have been traditional parities or differentials. The logic of such comparisons is often open to question—for any group, wage comparisons can be made in many directions. The unions will, of course, try to make those most favorable to a wage increase, while the management will make those least favorable. But once a particular comparison has been long accepted as equitable, it becomes very difficult to change. For example, in both the United States and Great Britain there are cities with a long tradition that policemen and firemen receive the same salary. At this equal salary it has sometimes been very difficult to recruit policemen, while there has been a long waiting list of candidates for posts in the fire department. Some public employers have reacted to this by trying to give a differential increase to policemen, but in several cases they have eventually been forced to extend the wage increase to firemen as well. The shortage of policemen could be alleviated only by increasing the excess supply of firemen.[6]

Nevertheless, established wage relationships sometimes change even among unionized workers. Where a traditional differential has been established in absolute terms (cents per hour) rather than in percentage terms, its relative value is eroded by rises in the general level of money wages until it no longer is sufficient compensation for the extra training or responsibility of the more skilled group, while its real value in terms of purchasing power is eroded by rises in the price level. In such cases, the more highly paid group may exert pressure to widen the absolute differential. Where the situation arises within one union, these efforts may take the form of attempts or threats to form a separate union. The special increases given to skilled craftsmen in some general wage settlements in the automobile industry are cases in point.

Demands of a particular group of union workers to achieve parity with a more highly paid group doing comparable work often have particular force because worker sentiment is mobilized around a concrete goal rather than simply a demand for "more." The force of such definitions of equity in wage structures in forming union goals should be contrasted with the outcome of maximization models, in which there is no room for concepts of equity. The successful drive of Canadian automobile workers for wage parity with the American employees of the same companies is an example of such a goal (where parity was defined as the same number of dollars per hour in the two national currencies for the same work).

In the long run the weight given by employers, the public, and other unions to claims for relative wage increases are likely to be influenced by labor-market conditions. The claim of organized nurses or schoolteachers that their pay is inadequate to compensate them for their long training will clearly be more convincing when there is a shortage of labor in these professions than when there is not. But it is also true that a rather wide range of relative wages may be consistent with adequate supplies of workers to each of the trades concerned. These issues will be considered further in Chapter 11.

EMPLOYMENT GOALS AND FEATHERBEDDING

We have been assuming thus far that the union formulates its wage demands in collective bargaining on the expectation that the employer will be free to adjust his employment in response to whatever wage is agreed on. This amounts to assuming that the final position will lie on the demand curve for labor. Some unions, however, succeed in imposing rules that force the employer to use more labor than he would like to at the union wage; in other words, the employer is forced off the demand curve to the right. This possibility greatly enlarges the area of union choice in the formulation of its goals.

The practices by which unions create additional employment are called *restrictive working practices* or, more commonly, *featherbedding*. Such practices are formalized into rules largely among craft unions, though informal equivalents may exist at the plant level in some industrial unions. Featherbedding takes a number of closely related forms. The union may require the employment of men who do no work (for example, musicians unions may require the employment of a local "standby" band when a well-known traveling band is engaged).[7] In other cases unions require unnecessary work to be performed; for example, the "bogus" rules of the typographical union make necessary the subsequent resetting of advertising material printed by newspapers from papier-maché matrices received from outside.[8]

In other cases a union may refuse to permit the introduction of technological changes; thus most locals of the typographers union have not allowed the setting of type by computers. Finally, the union may require that more men be used to do particular work than the employer thinks are needed. This is perhaps the most general form of restrictive work practice; an example is the musicians unions' rules on the minimum size of orchestras.

The case of requiring a minimum number of men for a task is analyzed in Figure 14, using as an example the requirement once enforced by the Chicago local of the musicians that an orchestra for a musical show must consist of at least 18 men.[9] The diagram shows the number of men who would be employed at each performance of a musical show at various wage rates. It is assumed that the musical would not be produced with an orchestra of fewer than 10 men; the demand curve is broken line *ABC*, which is vertical at an employment of 10 when the wage is $45 per performance or higher. The supply curve of competent musicians to any one producer in the absence of the union is assumed to be perfectly elastic at a wage of $15 per performance. In the nonunion case

FIGURE 14

A Hypothetical Example of a Featherbedding Rule

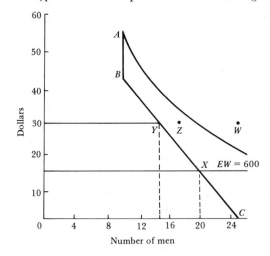

the producer would choose point X, using an orchestra of 20 men. If the union simply imposed a wage of $30 per performance, with no further requirements, the producer would choose point Y, using only 15 men in the orchestra. By combining a union wage of $30 with the requirement that the orchestra consist of at least 18 men, the union forces the producer to point Z, which lies to the right of the demand curve.

The union's ability to force the employer to spend more on his orchestra by a combination of wage demands and working practices must have a limit. At some point, the show would not be produced at all. In the diagram this limit is represented as a budget constraint consisting of a portion of the rectangular hyperbola

$$EW = \$600$$

where E is employment and W is the wage. The producer would accept any point to the left of this rather than not produce the show; to the right, the cost of the orchestra would consume such a large portion of his expected gross revenue that the production would be unprofitable. Thus if the producer were confronted by a requirement that he use 24 men at $30 a performance (point W), he would not produce the show. The area above the supply curve lying between the demand curve and the budget-constraint hyperbola is the area in which the union can choose a wage-employment combination that would be accepted. Since the demand curve and budget constraint will differ from producer to producer and will not be known exactly to the union, the point chosen by the union does not necessarily lie on the budget constraint of any one producer.

It is important to note that by specifying employment per task, the union does not determine the total amount of employment of its members either for the industry or for the individual employer. Neither does the union specify the ratio of employment of its members to all other inputs.[10] In general, the union requires that its members be employed in fixed proportion to some *subset* of other inputs, and there may be substitution against this whole subset. At the industry level the union's employment requirement will raise costs and prices and therefore will lower output (the quantity of product demanded). In our example above, these forces can be represented both by a reduction in the number of shows produced and by a shortening of runs (number of performances), since a larger proportion of seats must be filled to justify extending a run. There will be a tendency to use larger houses for musical shows (a change in factor proportions), which will also contribute to shorter runs. For these reasons, a requirement of a specified number of men per performance is not guaranteed to increase total employment. If the requirement were set too high, it could depress total employment at any wage below what it would be in its absence. A clearer case of the failure of a union work rule to fix factor proportions is represented by the rules of railroad unions on the size of train crews, which specify the number of men per train. The ratio of capital to labor can be increased (and has been) by having more and larger cars per train.

Since true featherbedding represents a conspicuous waste of resources, it is understandably condemned by management, economists, and the general public. In some cases, however, unions defend practices that appear to be featherbedding as necessary to protect the safety of workers or the public. The protection of union members from work hazards is an entirely legitimate union objective, and practices that in fact provide such protection should not be called featherbedding. An economist would nevertheless be inclined to insist that the added safety produced by these practices be obtained at reasonable cost—that is, it should meet the test of a careful benefit-cost analysis. The union is more likely to argue that life and health are priceless, to be guarded at any cost.

Featherbedding often has its origin in technical change that sharply reduces the employment of a particular craft. Such changes in employment may occur either because of new production processes in the industry where the craft is used or through the expansion of a competing industry. Thus television has reduced employment in the motion picture industry and the automobile and airplane have increasingly reduced employment in railroad passenger service, and unions in the declining industries have struggled to maintain employment. Union resistance to labor-saving technical change within an industry can often be moderated by careful management of change, which will minimize its effect in creating unemployment. This is much more difficult in the case of interindustry effects, since an enterprise in one industry is unlikely to be concerned with the effects of its decisions on employment in another industry. Technical change often produces losses for investors who have invested in equipment and skills that are made obsolete. Where the investment is embodied in people rather than in machines, the human problems it causes are more severe and less tractable. Those outside the union movement cannot condone a position that blocks technical progress, but they can approve one that uses some of the fruits of progress to give reasonable compensation to workers for the loss of their livelihood.

NOTES

1. This diagram has been adapted from Allan M. Cartter, *The Theory of Wages and Employment* (Homewood, Ill.: Irwin, 1959), p. 80. The slope of the supply curve has been changed for simplicity. It should be emphasized that Cartter presents the model only for discussion and does not believe it to be the most plausible one.
2. See A. Rees and G. P. Shultz, *Workers and Wages in an Urban Labor Market* (Chicago: University of Chicago Press, 1970), chap. 10.
3. Such functions are drawn in Cartter, pp. 86–94.
4. This paragraph is based on the unpublished doctoral dissertation of Hervey Juris, Graduate School of Business, University of Chicago.
5. See O. Ashenfelter and G. E. Johnson, "Bargaining Theory, Trade Unions, and Industrial Strike Activity," *American Economic Review* 59 (March 1969); and Daniel Hamermesh, "Wage Bargains, Threshold Effects and the Phillips Curve," *Quarterly Journal of Economics* (August 1970) .
6. See H. A. Turner, "Inflation and Wage Differentials in Great Britain," in J. T. Dunlop, ed., *The Theory of Wage Determination* (London: Macmillan, 1964) , p. 124; and E. J. Devine, "Manpower Shortages in Local Government Employment," *American Economic Review* 59 (May 1969) , 543.
7. For a discussion of working rules of the American Federation of Musicians as of 1948, see Vern Countryman, "The Organized Musicians," *Chicago Law Review* 16 (1948), pt. 1, 56–58, and pt. 2, 239–297. Reprinted in Paul A. Weinstein, ed., *Featherbedding and Technological Change* (Boston: Heath, 1965) .
8. For a classic discussion of this long-standing practice, see George E. Barnett, "The Printers," *American Economic Association Quarterly*, Third Series 10, no. 3 (October 1909), 435–819. Portions reprinted in Weinstein.
9. See Countryman, p. 31, footnote 43.
10. This suggests that much of the diagrammatic analysis of cases in which the union is said to specify either the level of employment or the ratio of employment to all other inputs represents wasted ingenuity. For example, see the articles by Weinstein and by N. S. Simler in Weinstein.

The Bargaining Process

THE SOURCES
OF BARGAINING POWER

The power of unions to wrest concessions from employers is based almost entirely on the strike—the concerted withdrawal of labor by all or some of the members of a union. Occasionally a slowdown or partial strike is used in place of an ordinary strike. Union members "work to rule" and reduce normal output by scrupulous observance of all regulations, or they refuse to perform certain functions normally part of their job even though they continue to perform others. The purpose of strikes and slowdowns is, of course, to impose costs on the employer through loss of output, profits, and customers if he does not accede to union demands. At the same time a full strike, as distinguished from a slowdown, also involves costs to the union, because members do not receive wages while on strike and the strike benefits sometimes paid in lieu of wages come from union funds.

The alternative sources of union power are political action, boycotts, and control of labor supply. Some government unions, such as the letter carriers, win wage gains through influence in Congress. Consumer boycotts have generally been weak weapons for unions, though they have recently been used with success by the United Farm Workers in organizing California vineyards. The secondary labor boycott is really a strike by a union not involved in the bargaining. True union control of labor supply through control of all opportunities to learn a skill is very rare. In most cases unions prevent nonunion members from working for union employers through an implicit threat to strike if nonunion members are employed.

On the employer side, there are three possible sources of bargaining power that permit employers to win some strikes. The strongest is the ability to replace strikers with other workers—called strikebreakers or scabs by the unions. This is now rare practice among large employers but may still be used at times, especially by small employers in areas where unions are weak. A more common practice is to carry on production operations, perhaps on a somewhat limited scale, by using managerial, supervisory, and clerical workers outside their usual occupations. This method has been used by utility companies, petroleum refineries, and retail stores. Where a company cannot carry on operations during a strike, its bargaining power depends largely on its financial resources—its ability to survive the losses imposed by the strike.

As all this implies, the balance of bargaining power differs greatly in different bargaining situations. At one extreme is the typical situation of the construction craft unions, where struck employers can have their jobs closed down for months while the strikers are working at good wages in some other nearby town. In such a case the fragmentation of bargaining units works to the advantage of the union. At the opposite extreme is the telephone company or electric utility where management and supervisory personnel can carry on the bulk of normal operations for months while strikers are out of work. Between these extremes lie the more usual cases in which strikes impose relatively equal losses on both parties.

It should also be mentioned that some employers may agree to union demands without ever engaging in negotiations. In the early days of unions, this occurred when unions unilaterally determined a pay scale. Today it usually occurs when a union extends a bargain reached elsewhere to employers who were not party to it. These employers regard it as certain that the union will strike if they do not accept the terms proposed, and regard the costs of a strike as clearly in excess of the probable gains from holding out.

MODELS
OF THE BARGAINING PROCESS

Economists have long been interested in formulating models of the bargaining process, or bargaining theories, applicable to union–management negotiations. This has proved to be an extremely difficult task. The factors that determine the outcome of the collective bargaining process are so varied and complex that it is exceedingly hard to devise models that are both realistic and manageable.

There are important differences between collective bargaining and the situations considered in more general bargaining models used in the theory of bilateral monopoly or the theory of games. For example, it is an important aspect of many bargaining models that the parties may permanently cease to deal with each other if the outcome is unsatisfactory to one of them. Suppose that Smith puts his house up for sale at $25,000 and that Jones offers him $23,000. They may then bargain over the difference with two possible outcomes—that a sale is agreed upon or that it is not. If Jones is secretly prepared to go as high as $24,500 and Smith is really willing to accept $23,500, then there is a zone of $1,000 within which the bargaining can go on; the exact terms of the sale will depend on the bargaining skill and tactics of the negotiators. However, if Jones has a firm upper limit of $24,000 and Smith is completely unwilling to accept less than $24,500, then no transaction will take place. Smith will find another buyer or continue to occupy his old house. Much of general bargaining theory consists in determining the limits at which parties will break off negotiations altogether.

This kind of bargaining model is of little relevance to collective bargaining, where the parties are generally forced to deal with each other permanently on some terms. Occasionally a small employer will go out of business rather than reach an agreement with a union. Occasionally a small union may be broken by a strike, and the employer will operate with nonunion labor. But the vast majority of negotiations must result, either before or after a strike, in an agreement that both parties accept. In this sense the zone of indeterminancy is enormous, because the option of no exchange is almost nonexistent.

Much of general bargaining theory deals with the division of a fixed stock, or of a flow of constant size, between two parties. Such models also are not usually applicable to collective bargaining. One of the most common reactions of an employer or an industry to a wage settlement is to raise the price of the final product, which passes on some of the cost of the settlement to third parties. Or the employer may adjust his level of employment as a result of a settlement. Thus the terms of the settlement themselves influence the size of the revenue flow to be shared.

Moreover, most bargaining theory deals with cases in which there are only two parties to the bargain, whereas in collective bargaining there are almost always, in reality, more than two. We have mentioned in Chapter 8 that the goals or tactics of union leaders are not always acceptable to the members; the leader may find himself bargaining with the employer in one direction and with his own membership in the other. In addition, the public is often an interested party either because a strike would harm or inconvenience users of the product or service produced or because a generous settlement would lead to price increases. Such effects can bring about government intervention in negotiations, which often goes beyond mediation or conciliation and becomes another active force in the determination of the outcome.

The kind of bargaining model that is most easily expressed in precise terms deals with only one magnitude among the terms of settlement, such as a price or a wage. Collective bargaining, however, is frequently multidimensional, and a concession in one area of bargaining, such as union security, may be traded for a concession in another, such as wages. It also helps to make a bargaining model manageable if one assumes that the nature and outcome of bargaining in one period does not affect the outcome in the next. Again, this condition does not hold in collective bargaining. If a union that negotiates annual contracts has a long strike in one year, it will regard a new strike the following year as more costly, since its members will not want to go without wages repeatedly. At the same time, the threat of a strike may not seem credible if strikes never occur; thus a successful strike, by convincing the employer that the union is strong, can produce gains that last over more than one bargaining period.

Despite these formidable difficulties, some of the propositions of formal bargaining theory are applicable to union–management negotiations over wages, though they are less applicable to negotiations over other issues that may be regarded as matters of principle. The central proposition of the theory is that each party to the bargain compares its probable gain from a strike with the costs, and is willing to strike (or accept a strike) rather than settle if the present value of the expected gain over the contract period exceeds the expected cost. However, since bargaining always involves an attempt by each party to conceal its true position from the other and thus to create uncertainty, the expected gains and costs cannot be known in advance with any precision. Moreover, even in wage negotiations a particular kind of parity or wage relation will sometimes be regarded by one of the parties as so much a matter of principle or equity, or will involve such a firm prior commitment, that they will strike (or accept a strike) even when the expected present value of this behavior is negative for the current bargaining period.

Carl M. Stevens has pointed out that one of the functions of the statistical arguments so often made in wage negotiations is to inform the other party of the strength of commitments of this kind.[1] For example, a union might present figures showing that its members are paid less than employees of other firms doing similar work. The purpose of these figures could be to convince the employer that he will not be at a competitive disadvantage in the sale of his product if he accepts the union demands. In most cases, however, their purpose is to convince him that the union is prepared to strike rather than accept a position it considers unfair. By increasing the employer's estimate of the probability that the union will strike, the union thus increases the amount the employer will offer to avoid a strike.

The gain from a strike for the union is the discounted value of the difference over the contract period between management's best prestrike offer and the expected settlement that could be won by striking. For management, the gain from taking a strike is the discounted value of the difference between the union's last prestrike demand and the expected settlement after a strike. The two parties need not expect the same settlement, nor will they ordinarily expect a strike of exactly the same duration. A difference in the expected duration of the strike will produce a difference between the two parties' estimates of the probable costs of a strike to each of them.[2]

During a strike two forces tend to bring the positions of the parties closer together. First, the costs per day of strike to each party are almost certain to increase as a strike continues. Second, if negotiation goes on during the strike, it improves each party's knowledge of the true position of the other and thus reduces uncertainty. This combination of rising costs and improved information eventually leads to a settlement.

The costs of a short strike to a union may be very low if the members have previously been working steadily. They can draw on savings for living expenses during the strike and can buy some necessities on credit. Some members may be tired of work and have things they want to do around the house. As a strike goes on, savings are depleted, creditors become less willing to extend further credit, and the union's fund for strike benefits is drawn down. The most important projects around the home that use free time productively have been completed. Thus the costs of continuing the strike become higher in each succeeding week.

The costs of a short strike to an employer who produces a commodity rather than a service will be low if he or his customers can build up inventories in anticipation of a strike and draw them down during the strike. As the strike goes on, these inventories are depleted and sales stop. Customers turn to alternative sources of supply, with the danger that they will find them to their liking and not come back to their former supplier when the strike is over. Although the costs of a strike to both parties rise with time, there are many cases in which the costs rise faster for the union. This will be particularly true where the employer is a large corporation with great financial resources and where the strike involves all the members of a union rather than a small group who can be supported by those still working. The greater staying power of the large corporation has led to the generalization that unions tend to win short strikes and management tends to win long ones, and the recommendation that managements must occasionally accept very long strikes to establish important matters of principle.[3]

It is also clear that the cost of a strike to a union is higher when business is bad and the members have not been working steadily, while the cost to management is higher when business is good. In good times inventories tend to be low and there may be backlogs of orders, so that loss of output is promptly reflected in loss of sales. Since the union takes the initiative in calling a strike, the fact that relative costs are lower for the union on the upswing of the business cycle means that there are usually more strikes during this phase of the cycle than in the downswing.[4]

A DIAGRAMMATIC REPRESENTATION

Some of the arguments on the preceding pages are summarized in Figure 15, a diagramatic representation of the course of the parties' positions during a hypothetical wage negotiation.[5] Wages are measured on the vertical axis, with the old wage denoted by W_0. Time is measured on the horizontal axis. Negotiations are assumed to begin in week 0, six weeks before the expiration of the previous agreement. The union makes initial wage demand D_1. A week later management makes it first counteroffer, O_1. These initial

FIGURE 15
A Diagrammatic Representation
of Wage Negotiations

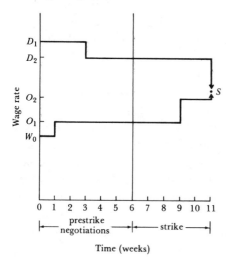

Time (weeks)

demands and offers are almost always further apart than the serious positions of the parties and are intended to stake out the general area within which bargaining will take place. The strength of the tradition that initial offers are understated may be illustrated by a recent court decision concerning the General Electric Company. For a long time the company followed a pattern of making a well-publicized initial offer and refusing to modify it during negotiations. This conduct was held by a U.S. Court of Appeals to constitute lack of good faith in bargaining.

After two more weeks of negotiation, the union reduces its demand to D_2, the lowest level it is willing to accept without a strike. Since management continues to reject this demand, the strike begins at the contract expiration date. Three weeks after the start of the strike, management improves its offer to O_2. Although the union does not accept this offer, the remaining gap is now narrow and negotiation proceeds at a faster pace. A final compromise is reached in the fifth week of strike at wage S, somewhat above O_2.

Clearly the number and timing of these moves or plays in the negotiation process will vary greatly from one negotiation to another. The positions of the two parties need not converge continuously. For example, management might make offer O_2 before contract expiration on condition that it be accepted without a strike, and if this offer is not accepted, management could return to O_1. Frequently agreement is reached without a strike. Sometimes negotiations break down and third-party assistance (mediation or conciliation) is needed to get them going again.

Since the parties eventually settle at S, it may be asked why they could not have arrived at this solution before the strike and thus have saved the costs to both sides. Part of the answer lies in the information communicated during the bargaining process. Management may initially have thought that D_2 was still an inflated bargaining demand rather than a serious one, and it may have been surprised by the union's willingness to fight for this demand and its slowness to retreat. If the union had accepted S without a strike, the members might have rejected the settlement thinking that they could gain more by striking, whereas after a strike of five weeks they would be willing to accept it as the best settlement obtainable. If it is conceded that the course and conduct of the negotiations as well as the objective circumstances of the parties influence the level of the final settlement, then it is hard to think of an operational sense in which it can be held that the settlement is predetermined.

THIRD-PARTY
INTERVENTION

So far we have been assuming that strikes end because of rising costs to one or the other of the parties, and this is usually the case. In some cases, however, the costs to the public or to other third parties rise much faster than those to the parties involved in the labor dispute. This is particularly likely to be true when the output of the struck enterprise or industry is a service or a perishable product rather than a durable product. A strike against automobile producers could go on for months without seriously inconveniencing the public, which holds a large stock of usable cars. On the other hand, a strike of bus drivers has an immediate impact on the public, for there is no way of using stocks to buffer the impact.

When the costs of a strike to third parties become very high, government or other neutral intervention in the dispute usually occurs. Three kinds of neutral intervention are used; in increasing order of forcefulness, they are mediation (or conciliation), fact-finding, and arbitration.

The role of a *mediator* in a wage negotiation is often to discover through private talks with each party separately a position acceptable to both that they have been unwilling to reveal to each other. For example, in terms of Figure 15, the union might have been prepared to accept S in week 8, but was afraid that if it had proposed it, management would have interpreted this as a sign of weakness and would not have offered O_2. The mediator who is able to say, because of his private knowledge of management's position, "I think management might agree to S if you would," can help to shorten the strike. Another important function of a mediator is to help get talks started again when they have been broken off. Mediation in labor disputes is routinely provided by the federal government and many state governments without cost to the parties.

Sometimes the parties cannot reach a settlement through negotiation even with the aid of a mediator, and in some procedures they then resort to neutral *fact-finding* with public recommendations. This step is included in the procedures of a number of states with laws regulating collective negotiations for public employees. Fact-finding is invoked if mediation fails to resolve an impasse. In general, the weaker party to a dispute may be anxious to have third-party intervention such as fact-finding because of the hope that the recommendations will bolster its cause, while the stronger party may resist intervention as long as possible. Attitudes of the parties toward intervention may depend also on how the fact-finder or arbitrator is to be chosen. Thus unions may favor fact-finding if a mayor or governor elected with union support is to choose the fact-finder.

The term *fact-finding* is something of a misnomer, since the fact-finder cannot in the limited time available justify a wage recommendation by making a detailed investigation of the underlying economic positions of the parties, without reference to their bargaining positions. Usually he inquires into the attitudes of the parties in an attempt to reach a compromise that might be acceptable to both of them if it were presented by him as a neutral. Both parties may sometimes be willing to accept a fact-finder's award because they do not have to take responsibility for it. For example, a union leader can tell his members that he thinks the fact-finder's award is too small but does not feel that a strike against accepting the award would be successful.

The last resort in the case of failure to reach agreement is *binding arbitration,* in which the arbitrator's decision can be placed in effect without the consent of the parties. Because this involves giving up their freedom of action, the parties rarely consent to such a procedure. If it is required by law, it may have the effect of keeping the parties far apart during negotiations, as each hopes that the arbitrator will split the difference between them.

Even fact-finding can have this result when it is used too frequently. Thus the regular recourse to emergency boards in railroad wage disputes has resulted in a situation in which the parties make few concessions in negotiations, and collective bargaining has almost been destroyed.

Conceivably this drawback of arbitration could be mitigated if fact-finders and arbitrators reduced the weight placed on bargaining positions in making their awards and did more to investigate labor market conditions as a basis for recommendations. Other ingenious proposals have been advanced to promote bargaining before intervention. One of these is to require the arbitrator to choose without modification between the final positions of the parties. This proposal should discourage the taking of extreme positions, but experience with it is still extremely limited.

The ultimate breakdown of the bargaining process occurs when there is a strike in defiance of an arbitration award and government invokes some degree of force against the strikers. Democratic governments have not yet evolved any satisfactory general method for dealing with such crises.

THE BARGAINING PROCESS
IN GOVERNMENT EMPLOYMENT

Until recently, bargaining in government employment had been rather different from bargaining in the private sector, because government employees were not legally permitted to strike. The main bargaining power of government unions was exerted through political processes—lobbying and efforts in behalf of candidates favorable to union positions. This is still the general situation in the federal government, although there have been a few successful strikes and slowdowns on the part of postal employees and air traffic controllers.

In state and local employment, strikes are increasingly being used despite legal prohibitions and even fines and jail sentences for union leaders. In a few cases the legal prohibitions are being removed. Organizations of government employees not affiliated with the AFL-CIO, such as the National Education Association and the Patrolmen's Benevolent Association, are becoming more and more like true trade unions. An increasing number of states are providing by law for collective bargaining of public employees.

Because of the growing importance of government unions, it is worthwhile to consider the nature of the bargaining process in the public sector. A government service financed by taxes (as distinguished from a government enterprise, like a transit system, that charges fares or similar prices for its services) has one great advantage over a private employer. Its flow of revenue is not halted by a strike; taxes are collected as usual. On the other hand, government negotiators face a number of important disadvantages. The union can use political pressures as well as the threat of a strike to win its demands. The government cannot move to another location to escape union demands, nor can it go out of business if union demands are completely unreasonable. Indeed, a number of government enterprises in such areas as transit were originally taken over by government because previous private owners could not operate profitably and pay union wages. Some observers feel that the balance of bargaining power lies more heavily on the union side in the public sector, but as yet there is little systematic evidence with which to test this view.

NOTES

1. Carl M. Stevens, "On the Theory of Negotiation," *Quarterly Journal of Economics* **72** (February 1958), 77–97.
2. Where two rational negotiators have the same expectations of the length of the strike and can estimate each other's costs, the outcome of the strike can in principle be determined in advance and the strike should ordinarily be averted. For a model with these implications, see J. R. Hicks, *The Theory of Wages*, 2d ed. (London: Macmillan, 1964), chap. 7. For a criticism of this model contending that it gives insufficient weight to uncertainty, see G. L. S. Shackle, "The Nature of the Bargaining Process," in J. T. Dunlop, ed., *The Theory of Wage Determination* (London: Macmillan, 1964), pp. 299–305.
3. See E. R. Livernash, "The Relation of Power to the Structure and Process of Collective Bargaining," *Journal of Law and Economics* **6** (October 1963), 10–40.
4. See A. Rees, "Industrial Conflict and Business Fluctuations," *Journal of Political Economy* **60** (October 1952).
5. This diagram bears some resemblance to the well-known diagram in Hicks, p. 143. The most important difference is that Hicks measures the expected length of the strike ex ante, while we measure the actual length ex post. Thus the diagram here is not intended to have any predictive value.

The Effect of Collective Bargaining on Relative Earnings

MEASURING UNION— NONUNION WAGE DIFFERENTIALS

Through the bargaining process, backed by the use or threat of the strike, unions raise the earnings of their members relative to the earnings of other workers. In recent years much effort has been devoted to estimating the size of this effect on relative earnings, with answers that vary considerably depending on the methods of estimation.

The basic difficulty of estimating the union impact on earnings arises because we cannot observe what the earnings of a union worker would be without the union. The best we can do is to observe earnings differentials between union and nonunion workers, taking care that the workers compared are as much alike as possible. However, these differentials may be a biased measure of the effect of unions, since nonunion employers often raise their wages because unionized workers have won wage increases. Usually the nonunion employer raises his wages to reduce the probability that a union will organize his own employees. In some cases he will pay his workers the full union rate and yet will prefer to remain nonunion, because this gives him greater flexibility in personnel policies and because his plant can operate while union plants are on strike. There is a similar gain from the absence of strikes to the workers in the nonunion plant. In addition, they save the cost of union dues—though they lose the services the union provides in such areas as processing grievances and establishing and enforcing seniority rights.

The direct effect of unions on nonunion earnings is now known in the literature as the *threat effect,* a term that indicates the threat of successful organization of the nonunion employer whose wages lag. Yet such direct threats are not the only way in which union wage gains can raise the wages paid by nonunion employers. In a tight labor market the nonunion employer may raise wages in response to increases in the union rate in order to compete with union employers in recruiting labor.

If we attempt to estimate the impact of collective bargaining by comparing wages in union and nonunion establishments in the same industry and locality, we will certainly underestimate it because of the threat effect; we may even find it to be zero. We are therefore forced to make wider comparisons, which leads to a greater need for corrections for differences between the groups of employees being compared. For example, we might compare different cities in which the same occupation was or was not unionized, correcting for other forces that affect the general wage levels of these cities.[1] Even this device does not remove threat effects entirely, for employers in one city might feel threatened by the growth of unions in another.

Where there are many employers in each market, they can be compared in another way. Instead of classifying markets as union or nonunion, we can estimate earnings as a function of, among other things, the percentage of workers who are covered by bargaining. Such a function is shown in Figure 16. The vertical axis of this figure measures the relative wage effect—the union wage minus the nonunion wage, divided by the nonunion wage,

$$\frac{U - N}{N}$$

FIGURE 16
The Relation Between Degree of Organization
and Union Influence on the Relative Wage

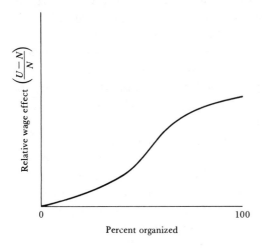

Percent organized

—or 1 plus the percentage by which the union raises the earnings of its members. The horizontal axis measures the extent to which the market is organized. The nature of the relevant market will vary from case to case, but it is better thought of as a product market than a labor market. In a local industry like building construction, the relevant market is a particular metropolitan area; in an industry with a national product market such as hosiery, it is the entire national industry.

There is reason to suppose that the union-effect function is not linear; rather, it is likely to be flattest at the two extremes. When the portion of the market organized is very small, the union will generally have little effect. If wages are an important element in costs, attempts to raise the wages paid by the few union employers much above the level paid by their competitors will put union employers at a severe disadvantage in selling their product. This will both strengthen their resistance to union pressure and encourage the union to moderate its demands. At the opposite end of the horizontal scale, the union will approach its maximum effect on relative earnings well before it reaches 100-percent organization because of the strength of the threat to organize the few remaining nonunion firms. It is in the middle range of extent of organization that the most rapid gains in relative wages are likely to occur as unionization grows. Some recent empirical studies show evidence of a curve of the shape suggested here.[2]

The discussion thus far has suggested that empirical estimates of the union effect on relative earnings are likely to underestimate it. However, not all the biases run in this direction. When unions impose high wages on an employer, the employer can respond in part by selecting workers who are better qualified than those he could attract at the lower wage. Much of this difference in quality cannot be measured in estimating the union effect on earnings; the result is therefore to overestimate the size of the union–nonunion wage differential for workers of comparable ability.

In some cases comparisons are made between workers in the unionized sector of the economy and workers in other sectors so far removed as to be beyond the range of the effective threat of organization. For example, agricultural labor, domestic servants, and the employees of small retail and service establishments might be included in the nonunion sector. Unlike the estimates discussed previously, estimates of this kind generally compare movements of wages through time rather than levels of wages from place to place at one time. In this case the effect of the union on the nonunion wage will generally be to lower it. The higher wages won by the union tend to reduce employment in the union sector and in those nonunion establishments where the threat of unionization is effective. This increases the supply of labor available to the rest of the nonunion sector, which tends to check the rise of wages there. If we consider the relative wage effect for the economy as a whole,

$$\frac{U - N}{N},$$

including in U those nonunion establishments that are subject to a credible threat of unionization, then the ratio differs from zero not only because the union raises U but also because it may indirectly lower N.

VARIATION THROUGH TIME
IN THE EFFECTS OF UNIONISM

The effects of unions on earnings are not uniform through time. Collective bargaining not only raises wages but also makes them more rigid by fixing them for definite periods. The length of the typical American collective agreement is from one to three years. Agreements of more than one year either provide for annual re-openings for adjustment of wages only, or provide during the life of the agreement for wage increases whose size is determined in advance or is based on movements in the Consumer Price Index.

The revision of wages at fixed intervals has quite different consequences at different phases of the business cycle. In some circumstances it holds union wages up. During the early phases of a depression, collective bargaining agreements can keep union wages constant while wages elsewhere are falling. In periods of moderate prosperity and stable prices, unions may win more frequent wage increases than are offered by nonunion employers. On the other hand, in periods of rapid inflation the rigidity of union wages becomes a disadvantage, and nonunion employers may raise wages more frequently than union employers. If the size of the union effect on earnings is considered normal or average in periods of moderate prosperity and generally stable prices, then it tends to be abnormally large in depressions and abnormally small in rapid inflations. If the extent of inflation or deflation had been correctly anticipated by the parties to wage negotiations at the time of contract agreements, then the size of wage changes could have been adjusted to correct for their infrequency. The historical record therefore suggests that changes in prices expected by bargainers have generally been smaller than those that actually occurred.

Table 12, based on the work of H. G. Lewis, suggests the general size of the union effect on earnings and shows the way in which it varies with economic conditions. The estimates are from time-series regressions that explain variations in the ratio of wages between two broad groups of industries, one highly unionized for much of the period and the other always substantially nonunion. The highly unionized group includes mining, construction, manufac-turing, transportation, communications, and public utilities; the substantially nonunion group includes all other private industries. The extent of unionism in each group, as well as certain control variables, enter into the regressions; the estimates show the effect of differential changes in the extent of unionism on the ratio of wages between the two groups. As expressed in Table 12, the figures are estimates of the percentage by which average wages in an industry that is 100-percent unionized would exceed average

TABLE 12

Estimates of the Effect of Unions on Relative Wages, 1920–1958

Period	Estimated Effect (Percent)
1920–1924	17
1925–1929	26
1930–1934	46
1935–1939	22
1940–1944	6
1945–1949	2
1950–1954	12
1955–1958	16

Source: Calculated from H. Gregg Lewis, *Unionism and Relative Wages in the United States,* Chicago: University of Chicago Press, 1963, Table 64. © Copyright 1963 by the University of Chicago.

wages in a nonunion industry solely because of the effect of the union. Of course, the wages could also differ for other reasons, such as differences in average skill levels.

The table shows a dramatic increase in the size of the union effect during the depression of the 1930s, no doubt as a result of downward wage rigidity in union contracts. It also shows a sharp decline in the union effect during World War II and the immediate postwar period. This seems to reflect the failure of unions and management to anticipate fully the speed and duration of the wartime and postwar inflation. After 1950 the effect of unions grows, reaching 16 percent in 1955–1958.

VARIATION BY TYPE OF UNION AND LEVEL OF SKILL

We have been considering the average effects of unions on the relative earnings of their members. Undoubtedly there is considerable dispersion of the effect of unions around this average beyond that produced by differences in the extent of organization. Thus one might expect differences by type of union (craft versus industrial) and by the level of skill of the employees organized. Finally, there may be differences that depend on the structure of the product market.

It is often thought that unions of skilled craftsmen have greater effects on relative earnings than do industrial unions.[3] The basis of this expectation is Marshall's laws of derived demand.[4] A union whose jurisdiction is well organized will generally set higher wage goals in bargaining, the less elastic the demand for the labor of its members, since inelastic demand means smaller percentage reductions in employment for given percentage increases in wages. In the short run, at least, there are not likely to be any good substitutes in production for skilled craftsmen, and the union thus has more to fear from substitution in consumption than from substitution in production. But in this case, as we have seen, it is desirable to be "unimportant." If the wages of members of one craft are a small part of a total cost, then even a large wage increase will add only a small percentage to the total cost of a unit of output, and a price increase that reflected this would cause only a small reduction in quantity demanded and hence in employment.

For example, let us assume that the wages of carpenters make up only 10 percent of the cost of a house and that no substitution in production is possible. Then a wage increase of 20 percent for carpenters would add only 2 percent to the cost of a house, which would probably have little effect on the number of houses built. If, however, the wages of carpenters were half the cost of a house, a 20-percent wage increase would add 10 percent to costs, which would have a larger effect on the volume of home building.

The cases in which this set of factors works to the union's advantage are those in which one craft bargains completely independently of others (for example, airline pilots). On the other hand, where all crafts bargain together, or where one craft sets a pattern that typically spreads to the rest, then what matters is the importance of the craft group as a whole. Where this group is still fairly small relative to total costs, as in newspaper publishing, the situation remains favorable. Where the wages of all crafts are a large part of total costs, as in residential construction, even a small craft no longer gains from being unimportant.

There remains another sense in which it may be valuable to a union to be small. If a strike of a small group of workers can tie up a large enterprise, the pressures on the employer to settle on favorable terms are greater than in a strike of the whole work force. He can then avert a large loss in production at relatively small total cost. But this factor too is important only when the settlement does not set a pattern for other employees.

The best available estimates suggest that unions have not, on average, been more effective in raising wages of craftsmen than of other blue-collar workers. Frank Stafford has estimated the effects of unions on the relative earnings of males at 52 percent for laborers, 26 percent for operatives, and 24 percent for craftsmen.[5] More recent estimates by Orley Ashenfelter, based on a better body of data, give different levels, but the same general pattern. For white males outside construction, Ashenfelter estimates union–nonunion wage differentials of 12 percent for laborers, 14 percent for operatives, and 3 percent for craftsmen. In construction, the differentials are both larger and more similar by skill, but the direction of the differences is the same.[6]

The explanation of the inverse relations between union effect and skill probably lies in the leveling effect of union wage policies. Unions have frequently sought the largest percentage wage increases for the least-skilled workers (for example, by bargaining for equal absolute increases for everyone). They have also sought to eliminate interfirm and interarea differentials, and craftsmen may be underrepresented in the low-wage firms and areas.

THE ROLE OF COMPETITION IN PRODUCT MARKETS

Another very difficult question is whether unions win larger gains when the product market is monopolized than when it is competitive, assuming in both cases that the union has fully organized the market. A positive answer is suggested by looking at manufacturing industries, where the unions that seem to be strongest are in industries such as basic steel and automobiles, in which a large fraction of total output is produced by a small number of firms. On the other hand, outside manufacturing there are many strong unions in unconcentrated industries such as construction, trucking, and bituminous coal mining.

The assumption underlying the view that unions gain more in noncompetitive industries is that unions can somehow succeed in capturing monopoly gains. This view considers unions, in J. K. Galbraith's terms, as having countervailing power that offsets the monopoly power of the employer. The opposite view sees unions in unconcentrated industry as having original power. By raising costs the unions can raise the price of the product to the general level where a successful product-market monopolist would have set it in the first place. Instead of capturing monopoly gains from the employer, they create them by their own strength.

The idea that unions can capture monopoly gains suggests that a monopolist will not raise his prices by the full amount of a wage increase imposed by the union, but will instead pay part of the increase out of his previous profit margin. This would generally be true of a profit-maximizing monopolist, although the precise answer depends on the elasticity of demand for his product. In contrast, the price charged by a competitive industry would in the long run have to rise by the full amount of the increase in labor costs. However, this does not mean that unions are better off when they bargain with a monopolist, if "better off" is defined in terms of the probable percentage reduction in employment caused by a given percentage increase in wages. For the same underlying cost conditions, the monopolist will tend to have a higher initial price and a lower initial employment than a competitive industry; that is, he will generally operate along a more elastic portion of the demand schedule for the product. This means that the percentage reduction in employment tends to be larger.

If we consider the possibility that many monopolists or oligopolists do not maximize profits in the short run, we see that it is possible for a monopolist to allow some of his profits to be "captured" by the union, but several other cases are also possible. A monopolist could "share" his profits with the union by paying high wages in order to avoid incurring the displeasure of regulatory agencies or antitrust authorities, but he might also share profits with nonunion workers for the same reason.[7] Where a monopoly or oligopoly administers prices, these prices may be held below the level that clears the market in times of strong demand. The automobile and basic steel industries followed such pricing policies in the period 1946–1948, as shown by the existence of *gray markets* for cars and steel in which sales took place above list prices. In these circumstances wages increases won by unions can be used as the occasion to raise prices by more than the increase in labor costs, so that the new prices are closer to the market-clearing level. Far from sharing profits with the union, the employers in question make the union bear the onus of raising profits closer to their target levels when increases in nonlabor costs have been eroding them.[8]

MISALLOCATION OF RESOURCES
FROM UNION WAGE EFFECTS

Because unions change relative earnings, they also affect the allocation of labor among sectors of the economy and probably cause welfare losses (losses in total output) that result from the misallocation of labor. Figure 17 shows one way in which this reallocation can be viewed. It considers an economy with a fixed supply of homogeneous labor, S, that is unaffected by changes in relative wages. The economy is divided into two sectors, N and U, both originally nonunion. The demand for labor in these sectors is represented by the parallel lines D_u and D_n, which sum horizontally to D_t, the total demand for labor.[9] Initially the wage is set competitively at W_c, the same in both sectors. Employment is E_0 in sector U and N_0 in sector N. Sector U is then organized by unions, who through collective bargaining set the wage in this section at W_u. The number of workers employed in the union sector falls to E_1 when employers and consumers make substitutions against union labor and union-made products. If we assume

FIGURE 17
The Effects of Union Wage Differentials
on Resource Allocation

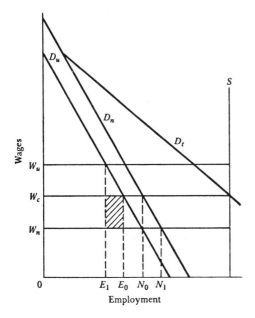

that the workers who have lost their jobs prefer working at the nonunion wage to remaining unemployed, the supply of labor to the nonunion sector increases to N_1, and wages in that sector, still determined competitively, fall to W_n.

The welfare loss arises because the workers who have moved from the union to the nonunion sector are now being used where their productivity is lower than before. The union sector has become more capital intensive and the nonunion sector has become more labor intensive. The area under each demand schedule up to the level of employment in that sector is the total product of the sector, assuming that the demand schedules are based on the value of the marginal products. The decrease in the total output of the economy is therefore the difference between the area under D_u from E_0 to E_1 and the area under D_n from N_0 to N_1. This difference is the heavily shaded rectangle between E_0 and E_1. Where (as in the figure) the demand schedules are parallel, it is equal to $\frac{1}{2} (W_n - W_u) (E_0 - E_1)$, or half the product of the wage difference and the employment change.

The analysis of the last two paragraphs is highly abstract and could be modified in many ways toward greater realism. The labor in the two sectors need not be of the same original quality; the two demand schedules need not be parallel, and nonunion labor markets need not be perfectly competitive. Such modifications do not all work in the same direction. In particular, the assumption that nonunion labor markets are competitive tends to overstate the welfare loss if in fact they are not competitive, while the assumption that workers who lose jobs in the union sector can transfer to the nonunion sector without prolonged unemployment tends to understate the welfare loss if the assumption is contrary to fact. Because of these offsets, the loss indicated by the diagram may be a reasonably good approximation to the result of a more complex analysis.

I have elsewhere made a rough estimate of the size of the welfare loss caused by the effect of unions on earnings and employment in the United States in 1957; the estimated loss is approximately 0.14 percent of the Gross National Product.[10] This estimate was based on estimates by H. G. Lewis of union effects on relative earnings and relative employment. Some subsequent studies have suggested that the Lewis estimates of the union effects on earnings may be too low, in which case my rough estimate of the output loss would also tend to be too low. However, the impression remains that the losses caused by the misallocation of labor to areas where it is less productive are rather small relative to losses that involve labor's being completely idle or nonproductive—that is, relative to losses from unemployment or from restrictive work practices.

NOTES

1. For two studies that use this technique, see Melvin Lurie, "The Effect of Unionization on Wages in the Transit Industry," *Journal of Political Economy* **69** (December 1961), 558–572; and Joseph Scherer, "The Union Impact on Wages: The Case of the Year-Round Hotel Industry," *Industrial and Labor Relations Review* **9** (January 1956), 213–224. A very thorough review of the literature on the influence of unions on earnings, and major original contributions to it, are to be found in H. G. Lewis, *Unions and Relative Wages in the United States* (Chicago: University of Chicago Press, 1963).

2. Two recent studies that have estimated nonlinear functions similar to that shown in Figure 16 and report that they fit the data better than linear ones are Victors Fuchs, *The Service Economy* (New York: National Bureau of Economic Research, 1968), chap. 6; and Sherwin Rosen, "Trade Union Power, Threat Effects, and the Extent of Organization," *Review of Economic Studies* (April 1969).

3. See, for example, Milton Friedman in David McCord Wright, ed., *The Impact of the Union* (New York: Harcourt Brace Jovanovich, 1951), p. 208.

4. See the discussion of these in Chapter 4.

5. See Frank Stafford, "Concentration and Labor Earnings: Comment," *American Economic Review* (March 1968), 174–181. These estimates are based on national cross-section data on earnings of individual workers from the Survey of Consumer Finances, which provides information on union membership.

6. See Orley Ashenfelter, "Discrimination and Trade Unions," in O. Ashenfelter and A. Rees, eds., *Discrimination in Labor Markets* (Princeton, N.J.: Princeton University Press, 1973).

7. For development of this notion that monopolists might divert profits to the purchase of nonpecuniary satisfactions in the labor market, see Armen Alchian and Reuben Kessel in National Bureau of Economic Research, *Aspects of Labor Economics* (Princeton, N.J.: Princeton University Press, 1962). For example, Alchian and Kessel suggest that monopolists will on average hire prettier secretaries than competitors, and at higher average wages.

8. For an analysis of such a case, see A. Rees, "Wage–Price Relations in the Basic Steel Industry, 1945–48," *Industrial and Labor Relations Review* (January 1953).

9. See Chapter 4 for the conditions under which it is appropriate to draw a downward-sloping demand curve for labor for the economy as a whole.

10. See A. Rees, "The Effects of Unions on Resource Allocation," *Journal of Law and Economics* **6** (October 1963), 69–78.

PART V

Wage Structure

CHAPTER 11

Occupational Wage Differentials

THE SOURCES
OF OCCUPATIONAL WAGE DIFFERENCES

The basic forces that affect the structure of wages have been reviewed in Parts I through IV. We turn now to an examination of the wage structure that is produced by these forces and to more specific factors that govern structures of particular kinds.

There are many structures of wage differentials: by occupation, by industry, by location, by race, and by sex—to list only a few. Since groups of workers who differ in one of these dimensions are unlikely to be the same in all others, particular differentials are seldom observed in pure form. In order to measure the differences in pay between groups that result solely from the way they are classified in one structure, it is necessary to standardize for differences in their other characteristics.

From a purely statistical point of view, one could start standardizing anywhere, but the economic significance of some wage structures is greater than that of others. Occupational differentials are perhaps the most basic of all, since they reflect differences among workers in levels and kinds of skill and in conditions of work. In a perfectly competitive market one might expect to observe almost no industry differentials beyond those that arise because industries use different mixes of occupations. (The qualification "almost" is needed because the nonpecuniary advantages or disadvantages of work may be related to industry rather than to occupation. For example, a secretary might prefer to do the same general kind of work in an insurance office rather than in an office that was part of a steel mill or an oil refinery.) We shall therefore start the discussion of wage structure with occupational wage differentials; in Chapter 12 we shall proceed to differentials by race and sex. Since it would become tedious to discuss each kind of wage structure separately, there will not be any separate consideration of the others.

The forces that determine the level of wages in an occupation change substantially depending on the length of the period being considered. In the very short run the number of people qualified for all but the least skilled occupations is fixed; if there is an increase in the demand for labor in an occupation, its compensation will therefore rise. Thus in the short run supply is inelastic and largely determines the number of people in the occupation, while demand largely determines their wage. Given adequate time for training, including in some cases time for the establishment of new training facilities, the number of qualified people in an occupation can be increased and the number who enter will depend on tastes, training costs, and expected career earnings. Thus in the long run the supply of labor to an occupation could be highly elastic. The height of the supply curve would largely determine compensation, while the strength of demand would largely determine the number of workers employed. It is the determinants of the long-run structure that are of most interest.

The basic outlines of the problem can be seen by making some limiting assumptions. Let us consider an economy with only two occupations, U and S. Occupation U is unskilled and can be entered at age 16 with no further training. Occupation S requires four years of formal training beyond age 16. (The people who train others to work in an occupation can be considered as members of that occupation to avoid introducing a third occupation, teachers.)

If all workers had both the same tastes and the same expectations about future earnings in the two occupations, and if all workers discounted future earnings at the same rate of discount, the supply of labor to S in the long run would be perfectly elastic at some constant differential above compensation in U. If the nonpecuniary advantages of the two occupations were equal, this constant differential, when discounted back to age 16 at the uniform interest rate, would be just sufficient to cover the cost of training. If the nonpecuniary advantages were not equal and workers preferred occupation S, the differential in money earnings would be less than enough to cover training costs. If, on the other hand, workers preferred U, the differential would have to be more than enough to cover training costs.

Differences among workers in tastes and expectations will cause the long-run supply curve for the skilled occupation to depart from the horizontal position it occupies in the case just considered. Where tastes differ, a small wage differential will suffice to attract into occupation S those with the strongest preference for this occupation, those who discount future earnings at the lowest rate, and those with the most optimistic expectations about the future size of the differential. Larger and larger differentials would be needed (for constant training costs) to attract additional entrants whose tastes and expectations differed increasingly from those just mentioned. The long-run supply curve to the occupation would therefore slope upward.

Discussion of the role of tastes in determining the long-run wage level of an occupation goes back to Adam Smith, who in a famous passage wrote:

> The whole of the advantages and disadvantages of the different employments of labor and stock must, in the same neighborhood, be either perfectly equal or continually tending to equality. If in the same neighborhood there was any employment evidently either more or less advantageous than the rest, so many people would crowd into it in one case, and so many would desert it in the other, that its advantages would soon return to the level of other employments.[1]

The nature of advantages and disadvantages of different employments must be specified to avoid the circularity involved in defining them after the fact as those things that make people change occupations. Smith, of course, went on to specify them so that his argument gives rise to testable hypotheses.

The advantages of an employment include not only the pay and any perquisites or amenities that go with it, but the prestige in which it is held and the satisfactions of working in it. If an occupation is disagreeable or held in low esteem, Smith argued, its pay must be higher to compensate for this. Moreover, this will be true even in long-run equilibrium, so that there will be no tendency for such compensating differentials to be eliminated by mobility.

Smith wrote as though all workers had the same tastes, so that everyone disliked being a butcher or a hangman, presumably to the same extent. In such cases, the size of the differential needed to compensate workers for doing disagreeable work is entirely independent of the strength of demand. However if tastes differ, this proposition will no longer be true. Suppose that all but 1 percent of the labor force considers being a butcher more distasteful than working in other occupations requiring the same amount of training, but that the remaining 1 percent does not. If the number of butchers demanded at a wage that does not include any compensating wage differential is less than 1 percent of the number of people demanded in all occupations taken together, it may be possible to fill all of the openings for butchers at this wage from among those workers who do not dislike the occupation.

More generally, if workers are arranged in order from those who like an occupation most to those who like it least, they will form an upward-sloping supply curve of the sort shown in Figure 18. In this figure wages are measured on the vertical axis relative to wages in other occupations requiring the same amount of training; the average of these wages is taken as unity. As the figure is drawn, if demand is small (curve D_1) this occupation will have lower pay than the reference occupations (W_1), while if demand is greater (D_2) it will have higher pay (W_2). If everyone dislikes the occupation, so that all of the supply curve lies above unity, there must be a positive wage differential, but the size of the differential will still depend on the strength of demand.

Even in this last case one may not observe compensating differentials if the general level of demand for labor in all occupations is low enough—that is, if there is substantial demand-deficiency unemployment—or if there is substantial unemployment among particular groups such as immigrants or racial minorities. Among the least agreeable occupations are many that require little skill,

FIGURE 18
The Determination of a Compensating Wage
Differential with Heterogeneous Tastes

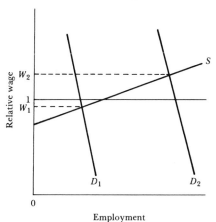

and in some of these there may still be downward wage flexibility.
The disadvantaged minorities and the long-term unemployed may
bid down the wages in such occupations, though they cannot in
others; or, by their willingness to do disagreeable jobs, they may at
least prevent wages in these jobs from rising with other wages. In
such circumstances the observed wages for disagreeable work may
be less than those for agreeable work requiring no more skill,
which is opposite to the result Smith predicted; but the composition of the work force in the two sets of occupations will be
noticeably different. A return to tight labor-market conditions
would produce shortages of labor in the disagreeable occupations
and would eventually lead to a reappearance of compensating wage
differentials.

A second component of occupational wage differentials may be
made up of rents to scarce natural talents, which are more important in some occupations than in others. Clearly, in the case
of professional athletes, actors, artists, and musicians, such rents
make up most or all of the differences in earnings between the
most successful members of the profession and the average
member. If average earnings in these professions are above those in
other occupations requiring as much training but less native
ability, this difference also consists of rents. But it is not clear
that on average there will be such rents. If new entrants overrate
their own chances of winning the large prizes or if they place high

value on the nonpecuniary attractions of such a career, many people of modest talent will enter. As their hopes of success fade, some of these people will not leave the occupation immediately because of the sunk costs of their investment in training. The result can be low rates of pay or frequent periods of unemployment that drive the average earnings of people in these occupations below those of other skilled occupations in which native ability is less important.

The most important basic component of occupational wage differentials is the one mentioned at the beginning of this discussion—the return on investment in acquiring skills. If a skilled occupation is to attract new entrants, the private costs of the training needed to enter it must be recouped over the recruit's working life with a rate of return equal to the return on other equally risky investments, or equal to the subjective rate of discount used by entrants in making their decision.[2]

THE HISTORICAL NARROWING OF SKILL DIFFERENTIALS

Historically, there has been a clear tendency for occupational wage differentials to narrow in percentage terms, and a large part of this narrowing can no doubt be explained by the fall in the private costs of training. Evidence of the narrowing of skill differentials can be assembled in two ways. One can take the ratios of earnings in skilled occupations to those in unskilled occupations and observe the movement of such ratios through time. This method is the easiest to understand and the most frequently used, though the results may be influenced by the particular occupations chosen for comparison.[3]

An example of the narrowing of skill differentials using the ratio method is given in Table 13. This shows in the last column the ratio of an index of union wage rates for bricklayers to an index of union wage rates for bricklayers' tenders, or hodcarriers. In the earliest year shown, 1907, the ratio was 72 percent larger than in 1967, and the decline is steady throughout the period. The occupations chosen are especially suitable for such a calculation because they are well defined and have been little affected by technological change.

A measure of the narrowing of skill differentials that has less

TABLE 13

Indexes of Union Wage Rates for Bricklayers and Bricklayers' Tenders, 1907–1967 (1967 = 100)

Date	1 Bricklayers	2 Bricklayers' Tenders (Hodcarriers)	3 Column 1 Divided by Column 2
May 15, 1907	11.0	6.4	1.72
May 15, 1917	13.0	7.9	1.65
May 15, 1927	28.3	18.6	1.52
May 15, 1937	26.5	19.2	1.38
July 1, 1947	42.6	35.1	1.21
July 1, 1957	70.9	62.8	1.13
July 1, 1967	100.0	100.0	1.00

Source: U.S. Department of Labor, Bureau of Labor Statistics, *Handbook of Labor Statistics, 1971*, Table 88.

intuitive appeal but that avoids selection biases is the coefficient of variation, a measure of relative dispersion, computed across all the occupations in an industry.[4] The historical narrowing of relative differentials is also apparent when this method is used.

Most studies of occupational wage differentials have dealt with skilled and unskilled manual occupations, where good data are available over a long period. Equally striking evidence of narrowing can be found by comparing the movement of earnings in white-collar and blue-collar occupations.

In 1899, according to the Census of Manufacturers, the annual earnings of nonproduction workers in manufacturing were 2.5 times as large as the annual earnings of production workers (wage earners). By 1963 this ratio had fallen to 1.5. The drop occurred despite the great increase in the proportion of professional and technical workers among the nonproduction workers. Since many nonproduction workers are clerical workers and the basic clerical skills are literacy and facility with figures, we may surmise that the fall in the private cost of primary and secondary education has been a basic force in narrowing the relative differentials.

The fall in the private costs of training has been of two kinds. First, the rise in the legal school-leaving age and the prohibition of child labor have largely eliminated juveniles between the ages of 12 and 15 from the full-time labor force. Since by remaining in school people in this age group no longer sacrifice potential full-time earnings, their forgone earnings have ceased to be a private cost of secondary education. However, these earnings are still a social cost, because society has decided to sacrifice current output in order to increase its investment in education. Second, more and more of the direct costs of secondary and, especially, higher education are paid by government or by the educational institutions rather than by students themselves and their families.

The fall in the private costs of secondary and higher education has of course contributed to the tremendous increase in the number of people receiving it. The result has been a sharp rise in the fraction of the labor force with the basic educational qualifications for professional, managerial, and clerical work. The same forces have also reduced the private costs of learning skilled manual trades. Apprentices can now enter apprenticeship at a later age, take fewer years to become journeymen, and earn a higher fraction of a journeyman's wage during their apprenticeship.

It has been argued by Gary Becker that the process of economic growth will reduce relative skill differentials even if there is no decrease in the private share of training costs.[5] The argument can be restated as follows. Consider an investment in training whose costs, C, are incurred in period 1 and whose returns, equal to the difference between skilled and unskilled earnings, $s - u$, are received in periods 2 and 3. (Increasing the number of periods will not affect the argument.) The internal rate of return, r, is defined as a rate[6] that makes discounted returns equal to costs so that

$$C = \frac{s - u}{(1 + r)} + \frac{s - u}{(1 + r)^2} .$$ (1)

Neutral technological progress then takes place, which permits all factor prices to increase by some proportion, a, and leaves all product prices constant. The real return to all factors, and the difference $s - u$ as well, is therefore multiplied by a. If the costs included in C were commodity costs (for example, books and supplies) rather than factor costs, they would not increase. To maintain equality (1), r would have to rise. This would induce further investment in skills, causing s to fall to some lower wage, $\hat{s}$. The new relative differential is

$$\frac{a(\hat{s}-u)}{au},$$

which differs from the old one only by the change in *s* and is therefor smaller. The new absolute differential $a(\hat{s} - u)$ might still be larger than the original one.

A different result would occur if costs consisted only of the salaries of teachers and the forgone earnings of students for an unchanged period of training. The left-hand side of (1) would then increase in the same proportion, *a*, as the right-hand side. There would be no tendency for *r* to rise and hence none for *s* to fall. Absolute differentials would rise to *a* times their previous size, and relative differentials would remain unchanged.

Becker realizes, of course, that teacher salaries and forgone earnings are a major part of training costs. However, he interprets neutral technical change as meaning an increase in productivity in *all* activities, including training. In this case, the length of the training period is shortened by the proportion *a* and the original argument holds for any mix of commodity and factor costs.

There can be no question about the formal correctness of this argument, given the definition of neutral technical change that is used. However, the historical change in technology has not been of this kind. The length of time needed to train people for skilled occupations, including both general formal schooling and specialized occupational training, has probably increased rather than decreased. This is because technical change has been most rapid in the production of goods—and of energy, transportation, and communication—and has been least rapid in the production of services, including education.

To explain the historical fall in the gross private returns to skill as measured by relative wage differentials, we are therefore forced back to the shift of training costs from the private to the public sector, since we cannot rely on the reduction of total real training costs through technical progress. This argument implies that if all the costs of training needed to acquire skill were paid by the public through a system of grants, occupational wage differentials would become much smaller and would be based entirely on compensation for nonpecuniary disadvantages of occupations and on rents to scarce abilities. These factors might be sufficient to justify some of the ordinary rules of wage and salary administration, such as the rules that a supervisor should receive more than the people he supervises or that additional responsibility justifies additional pay (on the assumption that scarce natural ability is involved in good supervision or that, other things equal, most people dislike taking responsibility). However, the size of the differentials considered adequate on these largely psychological grounds is less determinate than the size of differentials needed to compensate for private training costs, and the first set can be influenced by the extent to which an organization or a society has an egalitarian ethic.

In the United States during this century there has been another important force working to narrow skill differentials: the decline in immigration. In the years before World War I there was massive immigration from Southern and Eastern Europe of rural people who lacked both formal education and industrial skills. Their arrival must have tended to keep skill differentials large. This immigration was first interrupted by the war and then curtailed by legislation. Since 1923 immigration laws have kept total immigration low and within this total have encouraged the immigration of those with skills.

The role played by the European immigrant before 1914 has since that time been played to some extent by migration from farm to city. Like the last wave of European immigrants, the internal rural migrant has reached the cities with little schooling and no industrial experience. However, the force of this migration in keeping skill differentials wide in nonfarm employment must now be getting weaker with the declining size of the remaining farm population.

SHORT-RUN MOVEMENTS IN SKILL DIFFERENTIALS

There is a difficulty with all the explanations of the narrowing of skill differentials that has never been fully resolved. Although the forces discussed—including even the effect of cutting off immigration—should operate slowly, the historical narrowing is highly concentrated in two short periods: the two world wars and their immediate postwar inflations.

The narrowing of skill differentials during labor shortages can be explained on two grounds. The first has been suggested above in the discussion of compensating differentials. On the whole, skilled work is more pleasant than unskilled work, and a tight labor market will reflect the true extent of the compensating differentials needed to fill the less-pleasant jobs. The wide skill differentials in wages that are associated with the substantial levels of unemployment include a portion that represents the inability of the unskilled to earn the compensating differentials they should expect under full employment.

The other, and more important, argument about the narrowing of skill differentials during labor shortages has been put forward by Melvin Reder.[7] The differentials observed in the statistics are those between occupations or job titles and not those between individuals of standardized abilities. When skilled workers are hard to recruit, people who are not fully qualified are often promoted to skilled jobs. Some such people will become fully qualified through on-the-job training; others may be demoted later when demand slackens. But for a time at least, the quality of labor in the skilled occupation is diluted. In the completely unskilled jobs, however, where there are few, if any, qualifications to lower, the same process cannot operate. No one can be promoted to them from below, and workers can be attracted from outside the firm only by raising entry wages. The result is a compression of differentials between job titles but not necessarily a reduction in the premium paid for a constant standard of skill. As Reder points out, the same reasoning applies even when standards for promotion and hiring are not related to qualifications for doing the work. Standards of all sorts are relaxed during periods of labor shortage, and differentials unrelated to productivity will also tend to be compressed.

Although the explanation of the last paragraph seems adequate to describe the narrowing of skill differentials in wartime, it is somewhat troublesome because it is so independent of the forces that seem to account for narrowing in the longer run. It also raises the question of why the narrowing of skill differentials was not fully or largely reversed after wartime labor shortages were over. The best available answer seems to be that intensified on-the-job training during both world wars augmented the supply of skills and therefore lowered their relative price in the postwar periods.

Within the manual occupations, skill differentials are influenced by the policies of unions as well as by market forces. During the nineteenth century the role of unions in the United States must surely have been to widen skill differentials, since only skilled workers were successfully organized on a permanent basis. The extension of unionization to semiskilled and unskilled workers in mining, manufacturing, transportation, and public utilities, and the frequent use of across-the-board wage increases of a fixed amount, must subsequently have narrowed skill differentials in these industries. The evidence now available, which was cited in Chapter 10, suggests that outside construction, unions now have their smallest effects on the earnings of skilled craftsmen and thus on balance help to compress skill differentials.

The unskilled workers in services and small-scale retailing have not yet been unionized to any considerable extent. If an indirect effect of unionization is to reduce the employment of unskilled labor in the goods-producing industries, this could help to keep skill differentials wider than they would otherwise be in the service industries.

This chapter has been largely concerned with the forces that determine the equilibrium levels of occupational wage differentials. It may be useful to conclude it with a brief comment on the way in which disequilibrium situations are overcome. This process is not symmetrical for cases in which relative wages are too high and too low. When the relative wage of an occupation is too high, equilibrium is seldom if ever reached by cuts in the absolute level of compensation in this occupation. At best, its compensation will rise less rapidly than compensation elsewhere. As a result, there may be a long period in which there are more applicants for training places than there are openings. The training institutions can respond either by raising their standards for admission according to some criteria believed to be relevant to success in the occupation, such as grades in previous schooling, or by some other form of nonprice rationing (for example, by giving preference to the son and friends of those already in the occupation). In the longer run the pressure of applications may encourage the expansion of the number of training places, which will help to lower the relative wage.

Where the relative compensation in an occupation is too low, part of the adjustment may be made by lowering the standards for admission to training. However, it is much more likely in this case that compensation will also respond directly to the state of the market. In most cases, starting salaries will rise. Even when salaries are determined by a scale that is fixed for a number of occupations together, recruits in this occupation may be hired at a higher point on the common scale than other recruits, or they may be promoted along the scale more rapidly.[8] The brunt of the adjustment of relative earnings thus falls on the expanding rather than the contracting occupations. Moreover, there is a tendency toward the compression of the differences in pay between new recruits and their seniors when an occupation is growing very rapidly.

The kind of skill differentials discussed in this chapter accounts for much of observed industry and regional wage differentials because industries and regions differ in their skill mix. On the other hand, the race and sex differentials discussed in the following chapter can be very large between people whose skills appear to be equal.

NOTES

1. Adam Smith, *The Wealth of Nations* (New York: Random House, 1937), bk. 1, chap. 10.
2. See the earlier discussion of the supply of skills in Chapter 3.
3. For an example of this method, see Harry Ober, "Occupational Wage Differentials, 1907–47," *Monthly Labor Review* (August 1948) .
4. For an example of this method, see Paul G. Keat, "Long-run Changes in Occupation Wage Structure, 1900–1956," *Journal of Political Economy* (December 1960) . The coefficient of variation is the standard deviation divided by the mean.
5. Gary S. Becker, *Human Capital: A Theoretical and Empirical Analysis, with Special Reference to Education* (New York: National Bureau of Economic Research, 1964) , pp. 52–55.
6. There will in general be as many such rates as there are periods, but we may specify r as the most reasonable of these. For example, a negative r would not be reasonable even though it might solve the equation.
7. M. W. Reder, "The Theory of Occupational Wage Differentials," *American Economic Review* (December 1955) , 833–852.
8. See William G. Bowen, "British University Salaries: Subject Differentials," in his *Economic Aspects of Education* (Princeton, N.J.: Princeton University, Industrial Relations Section, 1964) .

CHAPTER 12

Wage Differentials
by Race and Sex

DISCRIMINATION
IN LABOR MARKETS

As everyone knows, women in general earn less than men, and blacks and some other minority groups (Latin Americans and American Indians) earn less than the majority group (other whites). The causes of these differentials are complex and controversial. In part they arise from current discrimination in labor markets and in part from differences in productivity, but the productivity differences are themselves the result of past discrimination in the labor market and in education. We shall begin by discussing current discrimination in cases where productivity is equal.

At the outset it may be useful to get some notion of the size of wage differentials by race and sex after controlling for some factors that could contribute to gross differentials, such as differences in age, location, and years of schooling. Table 14 shows estimates of hourly earnings in 1967, by race, age, and sex, for people with 12

TABLE 14

Estimates of Hourly Earnings of Adults by Age, Sex, and Race, 1967

Age	Male		Female	
	White	Black	White	Black
20–24	$2.43	$2.24	$2.07	$1.90
25–34	3.16	2.45	2.27	2.03
35–44	3.56	2.64	2.33	2.06
45–54	3.72	2.65	2.35	2.01
55–64	3.65	2.40	2.31	1.83
65 and over	2.93	2.22	1.86	1.66

Source: Robert E. Hall, "Wages, Income, and Hours of the U.S. Labor Force," Working Paper, Department of Economics, Massachusetts Institute of Technology, August 1970, Table 2-2.

years of schooling. The level of the estimates is based on New York City, but the data from which the estimates were made cover the 12 largest metropolitan areas. In every case the earnings of whites are higher than those of blacks, and the earnings of men are higher than those of women. The differences between earnings of white males and others at the same ages and educational levels are very substantial. We now turn to the question of why such large differentials occur.

The most common forms of discrimination are refusing to employ women or blacks in jobs for which they are qualified, employing them only at lower wages, or insisting on higher qualifications where they are employed at the same wages as others. Discrimination in the United States now seldom takes the form of paying lower wage rates to blacks than to whites or to women than to men working in the same job in the same workplace, in part because such practices are clear violations of federal law. The common forms are demanding higher qualifications for members of the minority group for doing the same work, or excluding members of the minority groups from the better-paid jobs. When different employers in a market offer different wages for the same occupation, as is almost always the case, members of minorities will be overrepresented in the work forces of the employers who pay the lowest wage.[1]

Data on the distribution of workers by occupation and color show that discrimination is greater, the higher one goes up the occupational scale. The underrepresentation of blacks in the best-paid occupational groups is to some extent a reflection of differences in educational attainment, but it is much greater than can be explained on this ground alone. Table 15 shows the substantial differences between races in the distribution of employment by major occupational groups. Nonwhites are underrepresented among white-collar workers, craftsmen, and farmers, and over-represented everywhere else.

There are three possible sources of discrimination in labor markets. An employer may discriminate because he himself is prejudiced, because he believes that his employees are, or because he believes that his customers are. However, an employer's testimony about the source of discrimination is not always reliable, since he may be tempted to deny his own prejudice by blaming others.

TABLE 15

Percentage Distribution of Employed Persons by
Occupation Group and Color, 1971

Occupation Group	White		Negro and Other Races	
White-collar workers	50.6		29.1	
Professional and technical workers		14.6		9.0
Managers, officials, and proprietors		11.8		4.1
Clerical workers		17.4		13.7
Sales workers		6.9		2.3
Blue-collar workers	33.7		39.9	
Craftsmen and foremen		13.5		7.9
Operatives		15.8		21.7
Nonfarm laborers		4.5		10.3
Service workers	11.8		27.6	
Private household workers		1.2		7.3
Other service workers		10.6		20.3
Farm workers	3.9		3.4	
Farmers and farm managers		2.3		0.7
Farm laborers and foremen		1.6		2.6
Total employed	100.0		100.0	

Source: *Manpower Report of the President*, March 1972, p. 173.

The term *prejudice* suggests an irrational dislike of a person or group. Discrimination can arise also from ignorance that leads an employer to underestimate the productivity of those he discriminates against. The distinction is of little importance in the economic analysis of discrimination, except that ignorance can presumably be corrected by supplying information, whereas prejudice cannot.

A THEORY
OF DISCRIMINATION

The concept of discrimination in employment has been given precise form by Becker.[2] If an employer can hire a black worker at the wage w, he is a discriminator if he behaves as though this wage were $w(1 + d_i)$, where d_i is a positive number that Becker calls the employer's *discrimination coefficient* (the subscript identifies the employer). An employer who refuses to hire a black worker at any wage, however low, has an infinitely large d_i. If d_i is negative, the employer discriminates in favor of a particular group; this behavior is called *nepotism* if the employer is himself a member of this group.

The extent to which an employer discriminates in the employment of minorities not only differs from employer to employer but also differs according to the nature of the work. (This suggests that a more complete model would specify a set of d_{ij}'s, where the subscript j identified the occupation). Where the duties of an occupation conform to the majority view of the appropriate social role of the minority—which is often that of doing menial or servile tasks—there may be discrimination in favor of the minority by majority employers. For example, until recently those American railroads that still operated dining cars invariably employed only black waiters and white stewards, though it would seem logical to fill openings for stewards by promoting waiters. This suggests that the white employers had a large positive d_{ij} for black stewards and a large negative d_{ij} for black waiters. In the case of the waiters, the term *nepotism*, with its connotation of kinship, is better replaced by the term *favoritism*.

Discrimination by an employer based on his own tastes and prejudices implies that the employer does not maximize money profits. On the contrary, he is willing to sacrifice profits by paying higher wages than he needs to or by accepting workers less qualified than others he could recruit at the same wage, in order to indulge his tastes about the composition of his work force. This is in direct contradiction to the traditional Marxist analysis of discrimination, which states that capitalists discriminate against or exploit minorities in order to increase their pecuniary profits. The present analysis does not deny that some whites, or even all whites taken together, make monetary gains as a result of discrimination in employment, but it asserts that the gainers are the nondiscriminating employers of blacks and the white workers who get the good jobs that, in the absence of discrimination, would have gone to blacks.

Becker has shown that in a competitive labor market the size of the wage differential between equally competent blacks and whites will depend on two factors. The first is the shape of the distribution of employers by the extent to which they discriminate; the second is the size of the minority group. A simplified form of his argument is shown in Figure 19, which represents an occupational labor market in one labor-market area. Total employment in the occupation is assumed to be constant. It is assumed further that the white

FIGURE 19
The Determination of Wage Differentials
with Discrimination by Employers

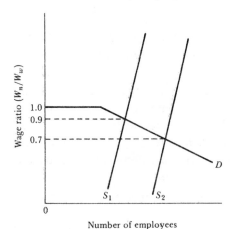

wage is fixed at unity and will not be depressed by a reduction in white employment. The vertical axis is the ratio of black to white wages, W_n/W_w.

The demand schedule for blacks, D, shows the total number of jobs that will be offered to blacks at each wage ratio. It is formed by arranging the offers of different employers in order by the extent to which they discriminate with those who discriminate least placed furthest left. The horizontal portion of D is the demand by nondiscriminators. The market wage ratio is determined by the position of the supply curve. If the supply curve is S_1, the wage ratio is 0.9; if the supply curve is S_2, it is 0.7. Thus, the larger the supply of minority workers, the lower their relative wage.

Those employers to the left of the intersection of the demand and supply schedules will hire only blacks in this occupation, since the market wage differential is larger than is needed to overcome their desire to discriminate. Similarly, those to the right of the intersection will hire only whites. Because those employers to the left of the intersection can hire black labor of standard quality at a below-standard wage, their money profits will increase, which should encourage them to expand. If all the firms were in one competitive product market, this would eventually enable the nondiscriminators to drive the discriminators out of business. However, the firms in a given labor market may be in many product markets, and some of these will have monopolistic positions in their markets. Becker's reasoning leads him to predict that in general monopolistic industries should discriminate in employment more than competitive ones, since monopolists can remain in secure positions toward the right end of the demand curve for black labor.[3]

It should be stressed that even perfect competition in all markets is not a sufficient condition for equal wages if all employers are discriminators, for in this case the whole demand curve lies below unity. One might object that under perfect competition black employers would enter the market and would have a competitive advantage, since they could be assumed to discriminate, if at all, in the opposite direction. In fact, this kind of competition is seldom a threat in markets serving white customers, for few black enterprises have the capital and entrepreneurial skills needed to enter these markets successfully and some white consumers may refuse to patronize them. To this extent, all competition in white markets is imperfect.

Figure 19 can be used as one explanation of the tendency for discrimination to be greatest where the minority group is a larger fraction of the total population. A striking example of this is furnished by the occupational position of orientals in the United States. In the West, where orientals made up 2.5 percent of the total employment in 1966, they were underrepresented in the best-paid occupations. In the North, where they made up only 0.2 percent of the employment, they were overrepresented in these occupations in comparison with whites.[4] This can be viewed as a case of two markets with identical demand curves, determined by similar dispersions of employer tastes, and different supply curves, like S_1 and S_2. Alternatively, it might be explained by making the tastes themselves (the level of the demand curve) a function of the numerical importance of the minority group, in which case one could get the observed result even if the demand curves in both markets were flat. The alternative explanation suggests that discrimination arises only against minorities large enough to be perceived as a threat to the position of workers in the majority group.

THE ROLE OF FELLOW EMPLOYEES, UNIONS, AND CONSUMERS

Some insight into the differences in the extent of racial discrimination by sex and occupational level may be gained by shifting our attention from prejudice on the part of employers to prejudice by majority fellow employees. The most important case is that in which the skills of the two racial groups differ, so that they are complements rather than substitutes in production. If most skilled workers are white, and if they prefer to work with white rather than black unskilled workers, the employer who employs blacks will have to pay his skilled workers a premium. He will be willing to do this only if the wage of unskilled blacks is below that of unskilled whites.

Kenneth Arrow has pointed out a particularly interesting case of this sort arising where people at one rank or level supervise or manage those at another.[5] The prejudice of whites against having a black supervisor is undoubtedly more intense and persistent than that against having black subordinates or coworkers. There are also usually more subordinates than managers. It is therefore expensive for employers to compensate all subordinates by enough to overcome their distate for being directed by a black superior. Since the best-educated members of the labor force are often in supervisory or managerial positions, the distaste of most whites for being managed by a black lowers the return on education for blacks. Many educated whites are highly paid managers, while very few educated blacks are. Similarly, if men (and perhaps some women) dislike being managed or supervised by women, there will be few female managers.

Where black and white workers have identical productive capacities, so that they are substitutes rather than complements in production, prejudice by white workers need not lower black wages. The result could be simply segregation, with some employers hiring only whites and others only blacks. The presence of fixed costs of employment would prevent such an outcome from being unstable if a small wage differential should arise in favor of one group or the other. An approximation to this result can arise within a firm, where races are sometimes segregated into separate work groups to reduce contact between them. For example, a firm that does not hire black production workers may hire black janitors, who clean up after other workers have gone home.

None of this is intended to suggest that an employer who discovers that his white employees are prejudiced must passively accept these tastes—he can and should actively work to change them. Employers and unions acting with skill and courage have often overcome resistance to the integration of work groups.

Wage differentials by race are affected also by the attitudes and policies of trade unions. Here a sharp distinction must be made between craft and industrial unions. Many craft unions have traditionally excluded black members and to a large extent still do, despite various public pressures designed to make them change. Blacks in the skilled manual crafts are therefore concentrated in the nonunion sectors of these occupations and have much lower average earnings than whites. Industrial unions, in contrast, have not excluded black members, in part because they needed the support of black workers when they organized their industries.

Some industrial unions (notably the United Packinghouse Workers and the United Automobile Workers) have been militant in fighting for minority rights. Even in industrial unions, however, particular locals may discriminate against minorities despite national union policy, and discrimination is most likely at the highest occupational levels. For example, in the steel industry many blacks are hired, but they are concentrated in the less-skilled occupations and in the departments where the work is least pleasant.

The overall effect of unionism on black–white wage differentials can be decomposed into two parts—the extent to which black and white workers are represented by unions and the effect of unions on the relative earnings of those that they represent. Estimates by Orley Ashenfelter suggest that for all male blue-collar workers, unions increase the earnings of black members more than those of white members. In the construction industry, however, blacks are underrepresented among union members, so that the two components work in opposite directions and the total effect of construction unionism is to lower the earnings of black male blue-collar workers relative to whites by about 5 percent. In blue-collar occupations in other industries, blacks are about as well represented in unions as whites are, so that the effect of unionism is to narrow the black-white earnings differential. For blue-collar males outside construction, the effect of unions is to raise the average wage of blacks relative to whites by about 4 percent; for the economy as a whole the average wage of blacks relative to whites is raised about 2 percent.[6]

Prejudice by consumers or buyers is important in occupations where workers are in direct contact with customers. The buyer of manufactured goods does not know the race of workers in the factory where the goods were made, but he can observe the salesman who serves him. Consumer tastes operate in both directions; indeed, black consumers may have a more intense preference for buying from black salespeople than white customers have for buying from whites. The first implication of this is that residential segregation produces segregation in employment in trade and services. Nevertheless, consumer prejudice may lower the relative incomes of blacks even though it operates in both directions. First, the policies of businesses that serve all neighborhoods, such as downtown department stores, may be dominated by the tastes of the white majority. Second, whites have higher per capita purchasing power, so black influence on the employment policies of retailers is less than the number of black consumers would suggest.

THE ROLE OF EDUCATION
AND EXPERIENCE

We turn now to that component of differences in earnings by race that arises not from current discrimination in labor markets but from differences in productivity. The clearest source of such differences is education, which differs between the races both in quality and in amount. Differences in the quality of education are hard to measure, but such proxy measures as are available (for example, per-pupil expenditures on schooling) suggest that schools with heavy black enrollment are inferior to others, and presumably were even more inferior in the past when most blacks were educated in the then legally segregated schools of the South. There are also differences between the races in educational attainment (number of years of school completed), though these are becoming smaller. In March 1971, the median number of school years completed by white members of the civilian labor force 18 years of age and over was 12.5; for nonwhites it was 11.9.[7]

The relation between educational attainment and discrimination in labor markets is complex. On the one hand, low educational attainment would account for some earnings differentials even in the absence of any current market discrimination. On the other hand, the available evidence shows that there has been, at least until very recently, more discrimination against educated than against uneducated blacks. This lowered the rate of return on education for blacks and induced them to invest less even where education was available on equal terms. Moreover, on average blacks have less capital than whites and cannot borrow on as favorable terms. This, too, should lower their investment in education, because they will tend to discount the gains from education at a higher rate.

Giora Hanoch has estimated private internal rates of return on education to males from the one-in-a-thousand sample of the 1960 census. For whites, the estimated rates of return on college education, starting at any lower level of schooling as a basis of comparison, are consistently 10 percent or higher. For nonwhites the

estimated returns are almost always below 10 percent, and sometimes substantially below.[8] Although the limitations of the data
used prevent putting much weight on the particular rates estimated
for nonwhites, the pattern of differences by race is unmistakable.
This pattern seems to reflect the concentration of highly educated
blacks in elementary and secondary teaching, the ministry, and
the lower or middle ranks of the civil service, and their conspicuous absence until very recently from the more lucrative jobs
in management, sales, and the professions in private industry.

Another source of productivity differences is that blacks have, on
average, somewhat less on-the-job training than whites. In part this
is a result of the higher incidence of unemployment for blacks,
which reduces their work experience. There is also discrimination
in access to formal programs of on-the-job training, especially
apprenticeship for the skilled trades. Most important, blacks have
been underrepresented in the occupations where experience has
the greatest value and the largest effect on earnings.

The analysis of discrimination in employment against women
does not differ in its essentials from the analysis by race, except
that there are additional factors affecting productivity. Women
typically do not have the strength to do very heavy physical work,
but the increasing mechanization of materials handling and similar
activities has greatly reduced the importance of this factor. Laws
limiting the weights that women can lift are designed to protect
women's health, but if the limits are set unreasonably low, the
effect is to keep women out of work that they could safely perform.

Most women marry and even more may expect to do so when
they are young, and this clearly affects the amount, timing, and
nature of their investment in education. During the period when
they have young children, many married women are out of the
labor force or work only part time. This lowers the return to
women on the kind of education designed to prepare them for a
specialized occupation. Moreover, the interruption of careers by
child rearing means that at any given age married women are
likely to have had less labor-force experience than men and
hence less investment in on-the-job training.

The responsibilities of caring for families also contributes to a
somewhat higher average rate of absenteeism for women than for
men. A survey of earnings of manual workers in Great Britain for
September 1968, showed that 22 percent of women lost pay

because of absence for all or part of one or more days, as compared with 15 percent of men, even though men had a somewhat higher rate of approved absences.[9] To the extent that one worker's absence reduces the efficiency of other workers, the loss of pay while absent is too small a penalty, and a profit-maximizing employer might want to reflect different absence rates in wage differences. However, a more just and more effective way of incorporating this behavior in pay structure would be to offer bonuses for regular attendance to all workers regardless of sex. There is no reason to penalize a woman with a good attendance record solely because other women are often absent, or to fail to penalize a man whose absence record is bad.

The various factors that may make the productivity of women somewhat lower than that of men are not nearly important enough to account for all of the large differences by sex in earnings and occupational structure. For example, a recent study by Ronald Oaxaca on pay differences between men and women explicitly accounts for the loss of experience resulting from married women's absences from a labor force because of having children and for differences between men and women in education and location.[10] Nevertheless, Oaxaca finds that most of the gross differential in earnings cannot be explained by these measurable factors. As in the case of racial minorities, it is clear that discrimination is involved and that a reduction in discrimination, by increasing the incentives for women to invest in careers, would diminish the present productivity differences.

One clear kind of evidence of the role of tastes and customs in the use of female labor is furnished by striking international differences in the use of women in particular occupations. For example, it is rare in the United States to find a female dentist or pharmacist, yet in some countries there are more women than men in these professions.

THE EFFECTS
OF LEGISLATION

In recent years there has been much legislation designed to eliminate discrimination in pay and employment. Where the legislation only prohibits differences in pay for the same work, as in some laws providing for equal pay for women, the effect could be to reduce the employment of women, which had previously been encouraged by pay differentials. This assumes that the principal barrier to increasing female employment is on the demand rather than the supply side of the market. If the barrier had been on the supply side, competition would presumably have already eliminated the pay differentials. Where the legislation also prohibits discrimination in hiring, its impact on minority employment is not clear. If equal-pay provisions are better understood or enforced than equal-opportunity provisions, minority employment could be adversely affected. If the equal-opportunity provisions are better enforced, the opposite result could be expected. Equal-opportunities legislation can also affect employers' inclination to discriminate, since laws can help to change attitudes. Some employers will evade such legislation or engage in token compliance; some will comply fully if unwillingly; still others will be persuaded by the existence of the law or by their experience in complying with it that their original prejudices were misguided.

There have been few empirical studies of the effect of legislation on discrimination. However, a careful study by William Landes of the effects of state Fair Employment Practices Acts concludes that "relative wages were higher by about 5 percent and discrimination lower by between 11 and 15 percent in states with fair employment laws compared with states without these laws in 1959." These results come from "cross-section regressions where differences among states in years of schooling, relative numbers, and urbanization were held constant."[11] The recent increase in the demand for highly educated blacks by business, government, and universities is also in large part an observable effect of government action.

NOTES

1. For evidence on these points, see A. Rees and G. P. Shultz, *Workers and Wages in an Urban Labor Market* (Chicago: University of Chicago Press, 1970), pp. 161–166.
2. Gary S. Becker, *The Economics of Discrimination* (Chicago: University of Chicago Press, 1957). The notation used here differs slightly from Becker's.
3. For a more complete statement, including some exceptions, see *ibid.*, chap. 3.
4. See Orley Ashenfelter, "Minority Employment Patterns, 1966," Princeton University, Industrial Relations Section, mimeographed, pp. 21–24.
5. Kenneth Arrow, *Some Models of Racial Discrimination in the Labor Market* (RAND Corporation, 1971).
6. See Orley Ashenfelter, "Discrimination and Trade Unions," in O. Ashenfelter

and A. Rees, eds., *Discrimination in Labor Markets* (Princeton, N.J.: Princeton University, 1973).

7. *Manpower Report of the President*, March 1972, p. 203.

8. See Giora Hanoch, "An Economic Analysis of Earnings and Schooling," *Journal of Human Resources* 2 (Summer 1967), Table 3. Similar differences in rates of return on schooling between black and white males have been reported by other investigators, although more recent data show smaller differences.

9. *Employment and Productivity Gazette* (September 1969), 824.

10. Ronald Oaxaca, "Male-Female Wage Differentials in Urban Labor Markets," unpublished doctoral dissertation, Princeton University, 1971.

11. William M. Landes, "The Economics of Fair Employment Laws," *Journal of Political Economy* 76 (July/August 1968), 507–552. The quoted passages are from p. 544.

CHAPTER 13

The Distribution
of Earnings by Size

THE SHAPE
OF THE SIZE DISTRIBUTION

So far we have been examining wage structure in terms of differences between the average wage levels of two or more groups. Such differences represent only part of the interpersonal variation in earnings, since there is always substantial variation in earnings within each of the groups being compared, and this is often more important than the differences between groups. For example, after a careful examination of the evidence Lydall concludes that not more than about 25 percent of the total variance of male earnings in the United States in 1959 is attributable to variance between occupations; the rest is variance within occupations.[1]

Another way of looking at the structure of earnings is to classify earners by the amount they earned in a year and study the resulting size distribution. When this is done, one discovers that such distributions have a characteristic shape. They have a single mode to the left of the mean and a long tail to the right—that is, they are positively skewed. Figure 20 shows one such earnings distribution. The frequencies at low incomes are rather large if part-year workers are included; if only full-year workers are included the lower tail contains fewer observations. More generally, the distribution of annual earnings reflects two components—the number of hours the earner works during the year and the amount he earns per hour. Each of these components is affected by both demand and supply forces. The worker can to some extent choose the number of hours he works and the type of work he does, and thus affect his annual earnings. However, the demand for his services sets limits to his area of choice; for example, he cannot work more hours if he cannot find an employer who will hire him for additional hours.

The shape of the size distribution of earnings gives rise to a problem that has concerned economists and statisticians for a long time. Many human characteristics, such as height, are distributed according to the familiar symmetrical normal distribution. This

FIGURE 20
The Distribution of Wage and Salary Income
of Male Full-Year Workers, 1959

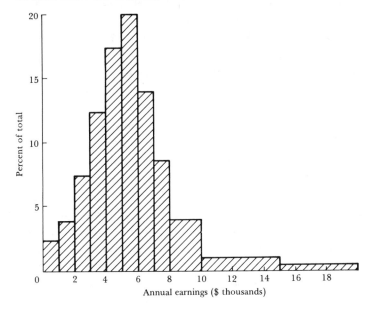

type of distribution is usually assumed to fit many kinds of ability, including mental ability, though the evidence on this point is by no means clear. Lydall presents some interesting material suggesting that the normal distribution of I.Q. scores is an artifact of test construction rather than a characteristic of the population being tested.[2] But if we assume a normal distribution of ability, why should it give rise to a skewed distribution of earnings? Such a bewildering variety of answers have been given to this question that the problem is no longer that of finding an answer, but rather of choosing judiciously among the competing alternatives.

THEORIES OF THE SIZE DISTRIBUTION: THE ROLE OF TRAINING

The alternative theories of the size distribution of earnings can be classified into two main groups: stochastic process theories and economic theories. The former, which we shall not consider here, generate skewed distributions of earnings from normal distributions of ability by the cumulative effect of random variation in fortunes through time. In other words, they view the actual distribution of earnings essentially as a result of chance, like the process that would produce winners and losers at a fair roulette wheel.

The economic theories are more varied, including many separate themes. Three of these are the effect of training, the interaction of separate abilities, and the hierarchical structure of large organizations. We begin by considering training, since the general outlines of the argument represent a continuation of the discussion of Chapter 3.

Suppose at the outset that all people have the same ability and that there are no nonpecuniary advantages or disadvantages in any employment, so that in the absence of investment in human capital, all workers would receive the same earnings. Then let us permit investment in human capital in two forms: schooling beyond the minimum school-leaving age and general on-the-job training (not specific to one employer), such as apprenticeship. We assume that some of the costs of this training are private costs, paid by trainees or their families, and that families differ in their access to capital, so that those with the easiest access to capital invest the most.

These new assumptions are sufficient to introduce both dispersion and skewness into the earnings distribution. Those who are getting on-the-job training will earn less than the standard earnings of the untrained during the period of their training, and they will form a lower tail of the earnings distribution. The larger number who have completed their training will be more productive than the untrained. In equilibrium this added productivity must, on average, add enough to their annual earnings over their (shorter) working life to permit them to recoup their investment with interest. Workers who have made private outlays for training will therefore form an upper tail of the distribution; the longer and more expensive their training, the higher their annual earnings after it is completed.

If differences in access to capital can be represented by differing interest rates, each of which is constant over varying amounts borrowed, then in this model everyone will have the same expected discounted lifetime earnings at minimum school-leaving age when his expected income stream is discounted back to that age at the interest rate applicable to him. This way of looking at differences in access to capital is unrealistic, but it serves to illustrate dramatically the effect of the convention of measuring income on an annual basis: There will be more dispersion and skewness in the distribution, the shorter the earnings period considered. A more realistic view of the capital market would have people confronted with upward-sloping supply curves of capital, not necessarily smooth, and differing among people in both steepness and level.[3]

The role of on-the-job training is also important in the variation of earnings with age. We have seen in Chapter 3 that earnings typically rise with age for younger workers, level off in middle age, and are lower for the oldest workers than for the middle-aged. The peak comes soonest in the least-skilled occupations. If all workers had the same schooling and had the same ability at a given age, the effect of the aging process would produce dispersion in earnings for people of all ages taken together. Some of this dispersion would result from their having differing amounts of on-the-job training, which accounts for most of the rise in earnings with age before the earnings peak (presumably the rest represents "maturity" not "produced" on the job). The second source of dispersion would be the changes in ability created by the aging process—the decline of physical and, eventually, mental abilities with advancing age.

Before we leave the subject of training, we should note that there can still be very substantial dispersion and skewness in the earnings distributions of people whose education is quite similar. Figure 21 shows the 1967 earned income of the Princeton Class of 1942, as taken from its reunion yearbook, *Twenty-Five Years Out.* Apart from the dip in the interval $25,000–$29,999, which is probably the result of small sample size, the distribution has the typical shape of earnings distributions. The median is $23,545, and the skewness is such that 15 percent of the observations are at earned incomes more than twice the median. Yet all these men had at least four years of college at the same institution, and all were about the same age. To be sure, some went on to graduate school and others did not, and they had different kinds of on-the-job training. Family connections no doubt assisted some to achieve

FIGURE 21
The Distribution of Earned Incomes in 1967
of the Princeton Class of 1942

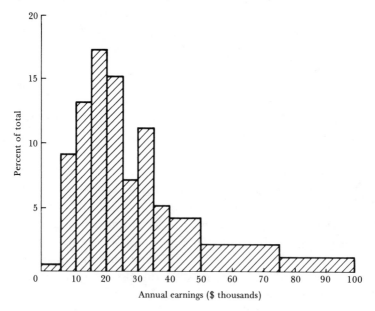

Annual earnings ($ thousands)

Source: "Twenty-Five Years Out," the 25th reunion yearbook of the Princeton University Class of 1942.

high earnings. But one is left with the suspicion that ability also plays an important part, and it is to ability that we turn next.

THE ROLE OF ABILITY

The model sketched in the preceding section will explain a good deal of dispersion of earnings, but it would require very large differences in access to capital to explain the great dispersion that actually exists. We therefore relax the assumptions of the model again and permit differences in ability. This will further increase the dispersion if ability is one basis of selection for scarce training places, but not the sole basis (which is a reasonable description of present selection mechanisms, such as college admissions procedures). There will be a tendency for those with the greatest ability to get more training and to have higher annual earnings after their training is completed, because of both their training and their ability. Among those with the same amount of training, those with the greatest ability will command the highest earnings. A policy designed to equalize earnings would therefore require compensatory education—that is, investing most in those with the least ability. For this purpose, ability should be defined to include the effects of childhood environment as well as genetic inheritance. It should also be clear that such an investment policy would not produce the highest returns on investment in human capital. As is so often the case, the goals of equality and efficiency are in conflict.

Once differences in ability have been admitted, however, it becomes very difficult to decide how far they affect earnings in their own right and how far they operate by enhancing the value of a given investment in human capital. The issue here is not unlike a question that arises in constructing models of economic growth: Is technological change entirely embodied in physical capital or is it an independent force? For many purposes, such distinctions may make little difference. Becker assumes, perhaps for convenience, that ability works entirely through increasing the productivity of investment in training.[4]

The difficulty mentioned in the last paragraph leads us to turn to models that consider ability directly. Although we have been talking of ability in general terms, it is clear that several quite different kinds of abilities can affect earnings—for example, intelligence, physical stamina, and manual dexterity. It has been shown that if each of the relevant abilities is normally distributed, but that if earnings vary with the product of two or more uncorrelated kinds of ability, then the logarithms of earnings, rather than the earnings themselves, will be normally distributed.[5] The lognormal distribution is a skewed distribution that fits actual earnings distributions quite well, perhaps better than any other relatively simple distribution. However, like the models based on investment in human capital, the multiplicative model of abilities is inadequate in explaining very high earnings, which are in general more numerous in actual earnings distributions than in lognormal distributions fitted to them.

Surprisingly little attention has been paid to the economics of the process by which ability is translated into earnings. The simplest case to start with is straight piecework. Consider an activity such as picking beans, where workers are paid a fixed amount per basket picked. If workers differ in only one ability (say manual dexterity) and this ability is normally distributed, and if all workers exert the same effort relative to their ability, then it follows that daily earnings will also be normally distributed. However, the operation just considered is a most unusual one because it involves no physical capital. For this reason, a grower will permit small children to work alongside their parents during the harvest even though they pick very little.

Let us now change the example to a factory job (say bench assembly) that is also paid by the piece and assume again that workers differ in the only relevant ability, manual dexterity, which is normally distributed. The employer will not retain the workers at the far lower tail of the ability distribution because they do not produce enough to cover the overheads of maintaining their workplace, such as the costs of capital, supervision, heat, and light. The employer may formalize this need for the worker to produce enough to cover overhead costs by setting a minimum production standard, say 25 percent below the average. A worker who, after a fair trial, cannot produce up to this minimum standard would not be kept on the job. In this case, although we have assumed a normal distribution of a single ability, the corresponding distribution of earnings has a truncated lower tail. A worker who is so unfortunate as to be in the far lower tail of all ability distributions relevant to any employment will be unemployable. If any ability (say intelligence) is relevant to all employments, a worker could be unemployable because he is in the far lower tail of this distribution alone.

Some specialized kinds of ability are economically valuable only in a small set of occupations, and then only when their level is much above average. For example, consider talent in music. Some amount of training in playing a musical instrument is part of many middle-class upbringings. Many of those trained must at some time have considered becoming professional musicians but had been discouraged by teachers who felt that they lacked sufficient talent. Only those in the upper tail of the ability distribution can hope to earn a living as musicians. Whether they choose to do so will depend both on the value they attach to the non-pecuniary rewards of a musical career and on their probable earnings in alternative occupations.

For these reasons the occupational use of a talent will not begin at a sharply defined point in the ability ranking, assuming that ability can be ranked; some amateurs will be better than some professionals. The importance of alternative opportunities in selecting the professionals can be illustrated by the high proportion of blacks among successful professional boxers. This need not reflect a racial difference in the distribution of the relevant abilities. It could arise solely because greater discrimination in other well-rewarded activities gives black boxers a greater incentive to turn professional and to invest in further training at any level of ability that has potential market value.

Let us now return to the example of musicians. A person who is very high in musical ability will continue to invest in training, but it is more the amount of ability than the length and quality of training that eventually determines his earnings. In general, the best schools and teachers will accept only the more promising pupils. The person with low musical ability finds this lack of ability irrelevant to his earnings in some other career and turns elsewhere for his employment. Suppose that there is somewhere in the employed labor force a person as much below the mean in musical talent as the most famous concert artist is above the mean. Where should we expect to find this musical moron in the earnings distribution of all employed persons? From all we know, we might find him at the median, since he may be average in all other abilities, and musicians are too small a part of the whole labor force to affect appreciably the median of the whole earnings distribution.

We have tried to establish so far that the process of choice of careers to accommodate tastes and talents would tend to produce dispersion and skewness in the earnings distribution, even if all abilities were normally distributed and if abilities did not need to be used in combination in any occupation. Very able people would receive high earnings that are in part a rent to specialized ability and in part a return on specialized training.

The skewness of earnings is reinforced by the way in which the demand for excellence determines the market value of people with exceptional talent. This is most obvious in the case of professional athletics. All baseball players with enough ability to play in the major leagues must be far out in the upper tail of athletic ability in the population as a whole; yet even among this select group, such superstars as Willie Mays earn perhaps ten times the minimum salary of a major league player. A similar process operates in music, art, and theater. The ten concert pianists considered by critics and audiences to be the best in the world must surely earn far more than those ranked 100th to 110th, if any ranking could be established that far down the scale. However, as Melvin Reder has pointed out, dispersion of tastes among consumers (lack of consensus about who is best) will narrow the dispersion of earnings.[6]

THE ROLE OF RESPONSIBILITY AND RISK

Although the examples used so far have been taken from sports and the arts, special ability may also play an important role in earnings in such professions as medicine and law and in such business occupations as sales and management. This leads us to consider a special theory of the upper tail propounded by Lydall.[7] It has long been known that the upper tail of many earnings distributions is well approximated by the Pareto distribution.[8] Lydall and Simon have shown independently that what is called the hierarchical theory of organization will generate precisely this distribution given the following assumptions: (1) that managers in a given grade supervise a constant number of people in the grade below them, and that this constant is the same throughout the organization; and (2) that the salary of managers in each grade is a constant proportion (greater than one) of the salaries of the people they directly supervise. It is argued that the salary is related to the post rather than to the man; that is, executives are paid mainly for responsibility "and that this criterion of payment is, in principle, quite separate from the criterion of ability."[9] This is shown by the general rule that supervisors are paid more than their subordinates.

The hierarchical theory is vulnerable at several levels. The supposed need for a reward for responsibility implies that people dislike taking it. This is often true, but it is also true that many other people enjoy responsibility and authority, perhaps in some cases too much. One can also question the assumption that ability is not the primary basis for selection for higher posts, except perhaps in family-owned businesses. The person who alone among hundreds of competing junior executives in a large corporation eventually rises to the presidency must surely have special qualities that account for his success, although they differ from the qualities that make a successful scientist or a successful salesman. In any event, a business that is not a monopoly would soon run at a loss if it selected executives without any regard to those kinds of ability relevant to managing a business well.

The most important difficulty with the theory is that it is too special, since it applies only to hierarchical organizations. Many earners of high salaries are not in such organizations. In the distribution of 1959, wage and salary income of males in the experienced labor force who worked 50–52 weeks during the year, 485,000 men (1.9 percent of the total) had earnings of $15,000 and over, which is the highest income class tabulated. But only 267,000 of the men in this class were managers, proprietors, and officials. More than 100,000 men with salaries of $15,000 and over were professional, technical, and kindred workers, and 59,000 were sales workers.[10] In both of these occupational groups individual ability seems more important on the whole than managerial responsibility.

Distributions of earnings with a Pareto-like upper tail can also be found within groups working in rather small organizations. Figure 22 shows the distribution of earnings of principals in architectural firms in the United Kingdom in the last accounting year before October 1967. More than half of the architectural

FIGURE 22
The Earnings of Architects
in the United Kingdom, 1967 (Principals)

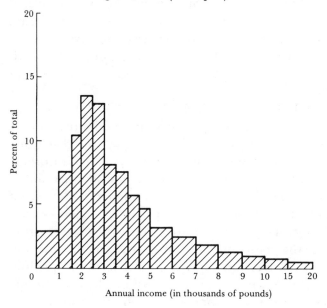

Annual income (in thousands of pounds)

practices had fewer than six members in the architectural team, yet the distribution is very like that predicted by the hierarchical theory.[11]

One final factor that produces dispersion and skewness in the earnings distribution will be considered: the willingness to take risk. Some careers involve much greater risks than others; in general, owning a business or self-employment in professional practice will involve greater risk than being a salaried employee. The greater the willingness of people in general to take risks, the lower the average return in such occupations and the greater the dispersion of the earnings distribution. We may expect to find many self-employed people in the lower tail of the earnings distribution who have been attracted into self-employment by the small chance of making a great gain. Balancing these will be the few who are highly successful. Clearly, ability plays a part in determining who succeeds, but chance also may play some part. To the extent that low income results from the deliberate assumption of risk through occupational choice, it may give somewhat less cause for social concern than when it results entirely from forces beyond the control of the individual.[12]

We have seen that there are many forces in the labor market that can help explain the shape of the earnings distribution, and all may play some part. Those that seem most important are differences in training and differences in ability. The understanding of these forces and the ways in which they interact has been impeded by the search for a single principle that can explain the entire earnings distribution.

NOTES

1. See Harold Lydall, *The Structure of Earnings* (Oxford: Clarendon, 1968) p. 104.
2. *Ibid.*, pp. 76–79.
3. For development of this point, see Gary S. Becker, *Human Capital and the Personal Distribution of Income: An Analytical Approach* (Institute of Public Administration, University of Michigan, 1967), especially pp. 3–5 and 14–16.
4. *Ibid.*, pp. 3, 16–20.
5. A. D. Roy, "The Distribution of Earnings and of Individual Output," *Economic Journal* 60 (1950), 489–505.
6. See "A Partial Survey of the Theory of Income Size Distribution," in Lee Soltow, ed., *Six Papers on the Size Distribution of Wealth and Income* (New York: National Bureau of Economic Research, 1969), pp. 216–217.
7. Lydall, pp. 125–129.
8. If we let N be the number of persons with earnings above some given level X, the distribution is given by $N = AX^{-\alpha}$ where A and α are constants. Pareto believed that α was generally in the region of 1.5, but higher values are often found. See *ibid.*, pp. 13–17.
9. *Ibid.*, p. 126.
10. See U.S. Census of Population, 1960, *Subject Reports, Occupational Characteristics*, Table 28.
11. The data for Figure 22 are taken from National Board for Prices and Incomes, *Architects' Costs and Fees*, Report no. 71, Cmnd. 3653 (May 1968), Table I (3). A very similar distribution of the earnings of solicitors can be found in the Board's Report no. 54, *Remuneration of Solicitors*, Cmnd. 3529 (February 1968), Table 10. The average number of persons per practice for solicitors was only 13.9, of whom 2.2 were principals. Some part of earnings of solicitors and architects represents return on investment in physical and financial capital. For the solicitors, however, the median amount of capital per principal was only slightly more than the median earnings, so that even at a high rate of return it would account for only a small part of the earnings.
12. For a much more extensive and formal treatment of this point, see Milton Friedman, "Choice, Chance, and the Personal Distribution of Income," *Journal of Political Economy* 61 (August 1953), 277–290.

Fringe Benefits

Compensation consists of two components: money wages and fringe benefits. So far fringe benefits have been brushed aside, and the discussion of wage structure has dealt entirely with the structure of money earnings. To remedy this deficiency, this chapter will briefly examine the structure of compensation in terms of its division into current money earnings and fringe benefits. Some treatments include in fringe benefits the value of paid leave, such as vacations, holidays, and sick leave. We prefer to regard paid leave as a reduction in hours of work covered by the analysis of Chapter 2. The corresponding definition of money earnings is then earnings per hour at work rather than the more common "earnings per hour paid for."

By fringe benefits we shall mean any part of compensation not paid currently in money to individual employees but paid by the employer on behalf of his employees, either individually or collectively. This concept does not include all the nonpecuniary benefits of a job, since some of these involve no explicit cost to the employer. However, it is somewhat broader than the national income accounting concept "supplements to wage and salaries," because that concept excludes expenditures on providing such amenities as subsidized cafeterias or recreation facilities. Some fringe benefits are required by law, the two most important being unemployment insurance and old-age, survivors, disability, and health insurance (social security). Others are provided unilaterally by employers or are determined by collective bargaining.

Compensation in kind has long been common in some occupations—for example, the provision of a manse or parsonage to ministers, or the provision of room and board to farm hands or domestic servants. With the growth of industrialization these traditional forms of payment in kind have become less important as a part of all compensation. In industrial societies compensation increasingly came to be paid currently in cash, a tendency that seems to have reached its peak in the United States during the 1920s. Since then there has been rapid growth of newer forms of noncurrent or nonmonetary compensation, particularly pensions and various forms of insurance, as shown in Table 16. The main task of this chapter is to explore some of the reasons for this

TABLE 16

Fringe Benefits as a Percentage of Total Compensation,
Selected Years, 1929–1969[a]

Year	1 Compensation of Employees ($ billions)	2 Supplements to Wages and Salaries ($ billions)	3 Column 2 as a Percentage of Column 1
1969	564.2	55.1	9.8
1959	279.1	21.0	7.5
1949	141.0	6.5	4.6
1939	48.1	2.2	4.6
1929	51.1	0.7	1.3

[a] Compensation of employees is the sum of wages and salaries and supplements to wages and salaries. Supplements include employer contributions to social insurance and employer payments for private health, welfare, pension, and insurance plans.
Source: U.S. Department of Commerce, Bureau of Economic Analysis, *Survey of Current Business,* **52** (July 1972), Table 1.10 and preceding July issues.

rapid growth. The importance of various kinds of fringe benefits is shown in Table 17.

The great advantage of current cash compensation is that it maximizes the worker's freedom to spend his income as and when he likes, and to make such provision for contingencies and risks as he thinks proper. In contrast, other forms of compensation determine part of his consumption pattern for him and, at worst, may be entirely useless to him. For example, group life insurance may be valueless to single workers without dependents (if they expect this status to be permanent). Offsetting these disadvantages are substantial economies of scale in purchasing such services as insurance. Because of saving in administrative costs, insurance carriers may issue group policies at much lower cost than individual ones, but they would not permit individual employees to opt out of the group for fear of creating an adverse selection of risks.

Economies of scale in providing nonmonetary compensation can

TABLE 17

Employee Benefits by Type, 1971 (Percentage of Payroll)[a]

	All Companies	Manufacturing	Nonmanu- facturing
Legally required payments	6.3	6.9	5.4
Old-age, survivors, disability, and health insurance	4.5	4.7	4.2
Unemployment compensation	0.7	0.8	0.6
Workmen's conpensation	1.0	1.3	0.5
Other	0.1	0.1	0.1
Not legally required	10.0	9.9	10.3
Pensions	4.9	4.1	6.0
Life and health insurance and death benefits	4.5	5.3	3.3
Other agreed-upon payments[b]	0.6	0.5	1.0

[a] Data are based on a survey of 885 reporting employers and cover the employer's share of benefits only. Since the reporting employers tend to be large, the percentages shown may be higher than for all firms. Payment for time not worked, profit-sharing plans, and bonuses are included in the original table and excluded here.
[b] Includes separation pay, meals furnished, discounts on goods purchased, and miscellaneous payments.
Source: Adapted from Chamber of Commerce of the United States, *Employee Benefits 1971*, Table 4.

permit an employer to cater to tastes of particular groups in the work force so as to lower his costs of recruiting and holding workers. For example, an employer in a warm climate who is the first in his area to provide a free employee swimming pool may find that this expenditure does more to attract new workers than an equivalent sum spent in raising wages. However, the attraction is only for people who like to swim. If more and more employers tried to follow this example, a point would be reached where pools were being provided for nonswimmers, and additional funds would be better spent on cash wages.

Employers may sometimes want to influence employee consumption patterns by providing income in kind in particular forms thought to be beneficial to the firm. In Britain it is common for employers who do not operate staff canteens (cafeterias) to give white-collar workers luncheon vouchers as a fringe benefit. These vouchers are accepted at restaurants in full or part payment for lunch. The company that operates the voucher scheme stresses in its advertising that employees do better work after a good lunch, though a more important reason for the scheme may be to permit employees to escape income taxation on a portion of their income. A careful study of the *truck system* of payment in kind in nineteenth-century British mining communities concluded that employer desires to influence consumption patterns (in particular, to limit expenditures on drink) were an important reason for the system.[1]

If an employer gives his employees freedom of choice in insuring against disability or providing for their income after retirement, he must refrain from aiding those who fail to provide for themselves. If an employer relied on his workers to purchase individual annuities to furnish income in their old age but was then moved by sympathy to provide later for those employees who did not do so, this provision would weaken the incentives to save on the part of the employees who had not yet retired. On the other hand, to force the retirement of a long-service employee who has no source of income (or only an inadequate one) might reflect badly on the employer or cause him to feel distress. Since even educated and intelligent workers may lack foresight in providing for the distant future or in insuring against unlikely misfortunes, governments and employers generally consider some compulsion to be a lesser evil than complete reliance on individual choice.

Most forms of fringe benefits either escape income taxation entirely or are taxed on more favorable terms than cash wages. For example, the personal income tax on employer contributions to pensions is deferred until the pension is received, when the worker will usually be in a lower tax bracket. Since the personal income tax has grown greatly in importance since the 1920s and is highly progressive with respect to wage and salary income, tax considerations go a long way in explaining both the growth of fringe benefits through time and their positive correlation with the level of earnings. Indeed, the tax factor is probably a more important cause of the growth of fringe benefits than all the other causes combined.[2]

We noted in Chapter 3 that employers who give their workers specific on-the-job training will want to encourage long service in order to protect their investment. A higher quit rate than anticipated would result in losses on investment in specific training, while a lower one would produce windfall gains. One way of reducing turnover is to provide additional fringe benefits to long-service employees or to make benefits contingent on staying with the firm, as in the case of nonvested pensions. Such practices have given rise to the fear of a "new industrial feudalism," to use the apt phrase of Arthur M. Ross,[3] which suggests both the paternal obligations of the feudal lord and the restricted mobility of the serf. Since specific training is probably correlated positively with wages, the desire to protect investment in training also helps to explain the positive correlation between fringe benefits and money earnings. The evidence that suggested the emergence of a "new industrial feudalism" is the long-term decline in quit rates in manufacturing. However, recent studies of the quit rate do not provide much support for the view that it is strongly influenced by the level of fringe benefits.[4]

The final force to be considered in the trend toward higher fringe benefits is the role of unions. Higher fringes may be paid in unionized firms for two reasons. First, unions may be better judges than employers of what employees want, and employees may want increasing amounts of security and amenities while at work. A possibly more important reason is that negotiated fringe benefits permit product differentiation by union leaders. The leader who first negotiates a new form of benefit, such as hospitalization insurance for dependents of workers, is a popular innovator.

The equivalent gain in cash wages would seem routine and in some cases insignificant.

The principal drawback of the rapid growth of private fringe benefits is that this growth has provided increasing security for those who are already most secure—the better-paid workers in the larger companies and the members of the stronger unions. The development of social insurance has been necessary to provide a modicum of security for workers in small enterprises and workers with casual employment.[5] Some of these, such as most farm workers, are still excluded from such important programs as unemployment insurance.

NOTES

1. See George W. Hilton, *The Truck System* (Cambridge, England: Heffer, 1960).
2. See Robert G. Rice, "Skill, Earnings, and the Growth of Wage Supplements," *American Economic Review* 56 (May 1966), 583–593.
3. Arthur M. Ross, "Do We Have a New Industrial Feudalism?" *American Economic Review* 48 (December 1958), 903–920.
4. See John H. Pencavel, *An Analysis of the Quit Rate in American Manufacturing Industry* (Princeton, N.J.: Industrial Relations Section, 1970).
5. Treatment of social insurance is beyond the scope of this book. For interesting recent treatments of some of the issues, see J. Pechman, H. Aaron, and M. Taussig, *Old Age and Survivors Insurance: A Tax and Transfer System* (Washington, D.C.: The Brookings Institution, 1968); and W. G. Bowen et al., eds., *The American System of Social Insurance* (New York: McGraw-Hill, 1968).

PART VI

Some Macroeconomic Aspects of Labor Markets

CHAPTER 15

Labor's Share in National Income

THE FUNCTIONAL DISTRIBUTION OF INCOME

In the last part of this book we look at labor markets in a larger setting and ask how they relate to the economy as a whole. The two main topics to be considered are labor's share of national income, which will be discussed in this chapter, and the general level of money wages, in the next. However, one cannot discuss labor's share of national income without simultaneously discussing capital's share, and one cannot discuss the general level of money wages without at the same time discussing the general level of product prices and the problem of inflation.

Discussion of income distribution is conventionally divided into two parts. The first is the personal or size distribution, and the second is the functional distribution, or division of income shares among the factors of production. For the first of these, a sharp distinction can be made between the size distribution of earnings, which was discussed in Chapter 13, and the size distribution of property income, which lies outside the scope of our discussion. The functional distribution is quite another matter. Whatever raises labor's share of total income must lower the property share, and conversely whatever raises the property share must lower labor's share, so that the two sets of forces are necessarily intertwined. Yet the functional distribution of income is usually considered as part of labor economics, because of the traditional interest of labor economists in changes in the size of labor's share and in the influence of unions on labor's share.

For our purposes, income can be defined as output during a particular time period (usually a year) minus the portion of this output that is needed to maintain the initial stock of real capital—that is, minus an appropriate allowance for depreciation and depletion. In other terms, income is the amount that a society could consume during a period without having less real capital at the end of the period than it had at the beginning. If actual consumption is less than this, the difference is an increment to capital that constitutes both saving and investment. For individuals, the concept of income is the same except that the definition of capital includes financial assets such as money, bonds, and stocks. These are claims of some individuals on others that cancel out for an economy as a whole.

In considering the personal or size distribution of income, one ordinarily includes only the part of corporate income that is distributed to stockholders as dividends, though in fact stockholders may also have unrealized capital gains that result in part from undistributed earnings. In considering the functional distribution, however, we include corporate profits whether or not they are distributed. A second aspect of the functional distribution is that we consider only the income arising in production, before there has been any secondary redistribution through taxes and transfer payments.

The property share of income includes the rent of land, interest, and profit. In a modern industrial economy the rent of unimproved land is a very small part of total income; most of what is entered as rent in national income accounts is actually a charge for the use of structures and improvements. At the outset we shall therefore treat the nonlabor share of income as though it were all a return to physical capital. Later on, monopoly profit will also be considered briefly.

THE CONSTANCY
OF LABOR'S SHARE

Table 18 shows the distribution of income in 1970 as reported in the national accounts. The compensation of employees (wages, salaries, and supplements to wages and salaries) makes up 75.6 percent of the total. This percentage has been rising through time—it was only 58.2 percent in 1929. However, there are two reasons for believing that this rise is an overstatement of the true rise in labor's share.

The less important of these reasons is the increasing share of economic activity performed by government. No return on government capital is included in national output or national income, although government activities do use capital; the whole output of government is represented by the compensation of its employees. The growth of government thus automatically raises labor's share of national income because of this accounting convention.

The more basic reason for distrusting the data on compensation of employees as a measure of labor's share has to do with self-employment. The data on proprietors' income, or income from self-employment, include a return on the labor of the self-employed and their families. To estimate the movement of labor's share, this return should be added to employee compensation. Since self-employment has been declining, the total labor share has

TABLE 18

The Distribution of National Income, 1970

	Billions of Dollars	*Percent*
Conpensation of employees	601.9	75.6
Proprietor's income		
Farm	15.8	2.0
Business and professional	51.0	6.5
Rental income of persons	23.3	2.9
Net interest	33.0	4.1
Corporate profits[a]	70.8	8.9
Total	795.9	100.0

[a] Before taxes and including inventory valuation adjustment.
Source: U.S. Department of Commerce, Bureau of Economic Analysis, *Survey of Current Business,* **52** (July 1972), Table 1.10.

been growing less rapidly through time than employee compensation alone.

It was long believed that when proper allowance is made for the decline of self-employment, labor's share of national income has been historically constant, and much effort was expended in explaining this supposed constancy. The most famous of these explanations is that production follows the Cobb-Douglas production function

$$P = bL^k C^{1-k}$$

where P is output, L is labor input, C is capital input, and b and k are constants. The constant k is labor's share, and the elasticity of substitution is 1.[1]

More recent estimates of changes in the functional distribution show a rise in labor's share even after full allowance is made for the labor component of self-employment income. This component can be estimated in three ways. First, the amount of labor furnished by proprietors and their families can be estimated and a wage imputed to it based on the wages of employees, leaving the return to capital in the noncorporate sector as a residual. This residual can be negative for some individual enterprises; that is, the total net income or profit of the enterprise can be less than the market value of the unpaid labor it uses. Presumably this is either a temporary situation or an indication that some people get large nonpecuniary benefits from being their own boss. Second, the amount of capital used in this sector can be estimated and a return imputed to it, with the labor share estimated as a residual. Finally, one can combine the two previous methods. Table 19 shows Irving

TABLE 19

Estimates of Labor's Share of National Income, Selected Periods, 1900–1958

Period	Labor's Share, Various Concepts		
	Asset Basis	Labor Basis	Proportionate Basis
1900–1909	69.4	67.8	67.9
1920–1929	70.8	71.5	71.2
1948–1958	77.0	77.3	76.8

Source: Adapted from Irving Kravis, "Income Distribution: Functional Share," *International Encyclopedia of the Social Sciences*, Volume 7, Table I, p. 134. Copyright 1968 by Crowell Collier and Macmillan, Inc.

Kravis's estimates of labor's share using all three methods; in each case labor's share rises substantially. Similar results have been reported for a number of other countries.[2]

THEORIES OF FUNCTIONAL DISTRIBUTION

There are two sharply different traditions in the explanation of the functional distribution of income, which have not yet been reconciled. The first of these, found particularly in the work of Professors Nicholas Kaldor and Joan Robinson at Cambridge University, sees functional shares as determined by differences between workers and capitalists in marginal propensities to consume, and by the Keynesian equilibrium condition that ex-post savings must equal investment. This line of reasoning can only be developed in the context of a complete Keynesian macroeconomic model, and since such models are outside the scope of this book, we cannot follow the Cambridge approach here.[3]

The older and still dominant tradition explains factor shares from the side of production. In its simplest terms it says that labor's share is the compensation of workers per man-hour times the number of man-hours of labor used in production, and capital's share is the return to a unit of capital services times the number of units of capital services used, where the prices or returns to a unit of each factor are equal to their marginal products. Under certain conditions, of which the most important is constant returns to scale, the payment to each factor of its marginal product would exactly exhaust the total product. If these conditions were not fulfilled there would be a residual (positive or negative) that would alter the share of the enterprise owners.

We have already looked at the division into factor shares of the output in a single production process (see Figure 7). In that diagram total output is the area under the marginal product curve up to e_0, the level of employment; the wage bill is the rectangular area e_0 times W_0, employment times the wage rate; and labor's share is the ratio of the wage bill to the total output. However, in Chapter 4 depreciation charges were included in the value of output and in the cost of capital services. In discussing the distribution of income, it is more usual to consider both output and capital's share net of depreciation.

The apparent simplicity of the production approach to factor shares conceals many difficult problems, and it is sometimes argued that these problems make the approach useless or circular. The income share of a factor can vary either because the quantity of it that is used changes autonomously relative to the quantity of the other factor, or because its price (marginal product) changes relative to the price of the other factor, which will induce changes in relative quantities. However, it is often difficult to separate factor incomes into quantity and price components. In the case of labor we have a measure of quantity (man-hours), though it is an unsatisfactory one if differences in the quality of labor are not taken into account. In the case of capital, on the other hand, it is impossible to obtain physical measures of inputs at an aggregate level and often even at the level of the firm, so that it is necessary to resort to proxies such as energy consumption or the horsepower of prime movers. Financial measures of the quantity of capital are either based on historical costs, which may not be relevant to current value, or they are themselves influenced by the market rate of return on capital (an asset yielding a perpetual net income stream of $1 is worth $20 when the interest rate is 5 percent, but is worth only $10 when the interest rate is 10 percent). This is most awkward when one wants to decompose changes in the value of capital services into quantity and price components. In Kaldor's view, these difficulties are so serious as to require the abandonment of the production approach. That view is not intended here; to point out difficulties is not necessarily to suggest that they are insurmountable.

When we examine historical changes in factor shares, we are of course not examining just the effect of changing the quantity of inputs with a constant production function. Technical progress is continually shifting the function so as to permit the production of more output for given quantities of conventional inputs. Almost all such progress is labor saving; much of it is capital saving as well.

By any measure of the quantity of physical capital, physical capital per worker has increased rapidly, which is what we would expect from casual observation of changes in production processes. Other things equal, this would lead us to expect an increase in the property share of national income, since there is now a larger

proportion of capital in the input mix. But this is quite the opposite of what has occurred.

A number of forces could resolve this paradox, of which two
seem most important. The first is the fall in the relative price of
new capital goods resulting from technical progress in their production. The relative price in question is the price of a piece of
capital equipment of given productive capacity, relative to the
wage of a given grade of labor. Since the return on physical capital
is expressed as a percentage of its cost, the relative price of capital
services will fall when this relative price of new capital goods falls,
even if the rate of interest, or rate of return on capital, is constant.

A second important explanatory force is the familiar one of
investment in human capital. Return on such investment, of
course, is included in labor income in the national accounts. Suppose that we think of output as produced by three factors rather
than two: physical capital, "raw" or unskilled labor, and human
capital. The last two of these are embodied in various proportions
in different members of the labor force. Nevertheless, we can think
of each of the three factors as having a separate price (or we could
assume that the rates of return on human and physical capital are
equal). An increase in the input of physical capital services per
man-hour would then not raise capital's share at constant relative
prices, provided that there had been a still faster increase in the
inputs of human capital per man-hour.

Since we lack a precise measure of inputs of both kinds of capital, we cannot be sure that this pattern of changes has occurred;
but it seems likely, given the rapid growth of technical, professional, and managerial employees as a percentage of the labor
force and the declining importance of common labor. (See Table
6.) Moreover, the same technological changes that bring new forms
of physical capital into use generally call for higher levels of skill
in the work force that must design, manufacture, install, and
maintain the new capital equipment.

THE EFFECTS OF UNIONS
AND MONOPOLIES ON LABOR'S SHARE

So far our discussion has proceeded as though the prices of factors
and the quantities of factors used were determined entirely by

market forces. Clearly, this is not always the case. In particular, the compensation of labor is often determined by collective bargaining. It has long been one of the stated objectives of the labor movement to raise labor's share through collective bargaining and thus to reduce the property share. Has this effort succeeded?

The question just raised is exceedingly difficult to answer. All of the problems that arise when one attempts to measure the influence of unions on earnings (and, as we have seen in Chapter 10, these are grave ones) are compounded when one attempts to measure the effects of unions on labor's share, because fresh sources of disturbance arising on the side of property income must be allowed for. The general answer given by those who have attempted such estimates is that no union influence on labor's share can be detected. The method most frequently used in such studies is to relate changes in the extent of unionization by industry to changes in the labor share of income originating in the industry.[4]

There is, however, no contradiction between the finding that unions raise the relative wages of their members and the finding that unions fail to raise labor's share, even within particular industries where they are powerful. One of the commonest management responses to higher labor costs is to increase the capital intensity of production methods—that is, to invest in labor-saving equipment. This means that the percentage increase in the wage bill will be smaller than that in the wage rate. Indeed, in some cases the long-run effect of a wage increase would be to *decrease* the wage bill; these are the cases in which the elasticity of demand for labor is greater than unity. The substitution of capital for labor also means an increase in outlays on capital services, for the new equipment must earn a reasonable rate of return. The combination of these effects may result in a labor share that is smaller, rather than larger, after long-run adjustment to a wage increase. This seems to have occurred in the bituminous coal industry, where higher wages have contributed to a rapid expansion of mechanization and the use of less-labor-intensive methods of production, such as strip mining.

Monopoly in product markets can also be expected to affect labor's share, but here the direction of the effect is less ambiguous. A successful monopolist will earn a monopoly profit over and above the going rate of return on the capital he uses, and this should decrease labor's share. However, monopoly profit is not, strictly speaking, a return on capital; it is a rent arising from the legal or technological position that created the monopoly and that prevents other firms from entering the protected market. For this reason increased monopoly profit, unlike higher wages won by unions, does not necessarily mean that inputs will be used in proportions different from those that would prevail if all markets were competitive. In the national income accounts, monopoly profit cannot be distinguished from profits that are a normal rate of return on equity capital or from the short-run gains that can arise when a competitive market is in temporary disequilibrium.

If a competitive industry were suddenly transformed into a profit-maximizing monopoly, protected from foreign competition by tariffs and with no fear of government interference with its position, one would expect prices to rise relative to marginal costs. Physical output and the use of all inputs would decline, the *value* of total output would decline less if at all, and labor's share of income would decline. The effect on labor's share need not be much different if the competitive industry were to become a regulated monopoly held to some "reasonable" rate of return on its total assets by the regulatory body, although in this case factor proportions might change. Whenever such an industry could borrow funds at less than the permitted rate of return on total assets, it would have an incentive to use more capital, and labor's share could decline for this reason.

All of this suggests that a possible logical reason for the historical rise of labor's share in national income could be a secular decrease in the extent of monopoly in product markets. However, there is no evidence that such a decrease has actually occurred. We are therefore left with the decline in the relative price of capital goods and the increase in investment in training and education as the two most probable causes of the slow, steady rise in labor's share of national income.

NOTES

1. See Paul H. Douglas, "Are There Laws of Production?" *American Economic Review* **38** (March 1948), 1–41.
2. See K. Heidensohn, "Labor's Share in National Income—A Constant?" *The Manchester School of Economic and Social Studies* **37** (December 1969), 295–321.
3. For a very lucid exposition of the model, see N. Kaldor, "Alternative Theories of Distribution," *The Review of Economic Studies* **23** (1955), 83–100. Reprinted

in B. J. McCormick and E. Owen Smith, *The Labour Market* (Baltimore: Penguin, 1968).

4. See Clark Kerr, "Labor's Income Share and the Labor Movement," in G. W. Taylor and F. C. Pierson, eds., *New Concepts in Wage Determination* (New York: McGraw-Hill, 1957); and Norman J. Simler, *The Impact of Unionism on Wage–Income Ratios in the Manufacturing Section of the Economy* (Minneapolis: University of Minnesota Press, 1961).

CHAPTER 16

The General Level of Money Wages

THE LEVEL OF WAGES IN A DEPRESSION

The topic of this chapter once would have been thought to lie wholly outside the realm of labor economics, but in recent years it has become more important in the labor economics literature than any other topic. Until the 1930s most economists accepted the view that the labor market determines the pattern of relative wages—or the wage structure—and determines the general level of real wages, insofar as these are affected by the size of the labor supply. However, the general level of money wages and money prices were not thought to depend on anything that happens in either labor or product markets, but to depend entirely on changes in the quantity of money and its velocity of circulation. In other words, in this view the economy can be decomposed into two separate sectors—the first monetary and the second real—with labor markets forming part of the real sector. All relative prices and the quantities of all real outputs and inputs (and hence all real incomes) are determined in the real sector. The monetary sector merely determines the nominal units in which prices are stated.

To be sure, the neoclassical economists had noted the downward rigidity of money wages, and they felt that this rigidity aggravated any temporary malfunctioning of the monetary sector by creating unemployment. Wages should be flexible downward, they thought, so that the real effects of a decline in the quantity of money would be minimal. If all wages and prices fell in the same proportion, output and employment could be maintained.

In contrast, Keynes argued that a reduction in wages during a depression is undesirable, because it would force a reduction in the consumption expenditures of workers, thus leading to a further decline in aggregate demand.[1] Wage cuts could also generate expectations of further reductions of wages and prices, leading to postponement of expenditures on durable goods by both consumers and firms, and this, too, would aggravate the depression. Finally, Keynes viewed reductions in money wages as inequitable, because the money incomes of rentiers (such as bondholders) would remain constant—which would raise their relative incomes if wages fell. In short, he saw the downward rigidity of money wages not as an imperfection of the economy to be overcome, but as a basic feature to be accepted and even welcomed.

Once the downward rigidity of money wages is accepted as a basic feature of the economic system, the level of money wages becomes in part historically determined, and money ceases to be a mere *numeraire*. A decline in demand (whether produced by a fall in the quantity of money or by an autonomous shift in the investment function) cannot lower all wages and prices proportionally. Therefore it must lower real output and employment. If some product prices are flexible downward, a decline in aggregate demand may even *raise* the real wages of those who remain employed. The real output of the system is determined by the level of aggregate demand whenever there is not enough demand to employ the whole labor force at the old level of money wages, while the price level is strongly influenced by the rigid money-wage level no matter how small aggregate demand becomes.

The Keynesian view of the general level of money wages in a depression is illustrated in Figure 23. The full-employment aggregate demand curve for labor is D_0, and the supply curve is SS.

FIGURE 23
The Labor Market During a Depression

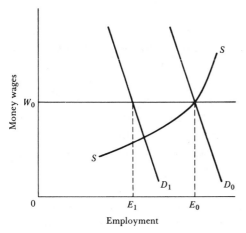

The reasons for drawing the aggregate demand curve with a downward slope were given in Chapter 4. It should be recalled that to draw a curve showing constant aggregate demand at different money wages, one must assume an offsetting change in some other source of expenditure. Together the demand and supply curves determine the money-wage level, W_0, and the amount of employment, E_0. Although there may be frictional unemployment at E_0, it is balanced by unfilled vacancies; thus there is enough demand to employ all those who want to work at the prevailing wage. Assume that there is then a decline in aggregate demand, for whatever reason (a fall in the money supply, a decline in government expenditures, or a shift in the investment function). The new aggregate demand curve, D_1, and the old wage level, W_0, will determine the new level of employment, E_1. If we abstract from any induced changes in the size of the labor force, the horizontal distance E_0E_1 is the excess supply of labor, or the amount of demand-deficiency unemployment.

Some Keynesian writers regard W_0 as forming part of the supply curve of labor up to E_0, and disregard the portion of SS to the left of E_0 because it is not accessible to employers. It seems preferable to regard all of SS as the supply curve and to regard the new equilibrium position as lying above the supply curve. This view calls attention to the willingness of the unemployed to work for less than the prevailing money wage—that is, to the involuntary nature of demand-deficiency unemployment. Regardless of which way the supply curve is viewed, however, the size of the excess supply is the same.

We next ask why the money wage is in fact rigid downward. In many cases this is because of trade unions—in the short run because wages are fixed by collective bargaining agreements and in the longer run because union negotiators will resist wage cuts. The British economy was well organized by unions at the time Keynes wrote, and this seems to be the reason he had in mind. However, similar downward rigidity in money wages can be observed in unorganized American industries (especially those dominated by a few large firms) in the period 1929–1932, before the rapid growth of industrial unionism in manufacturing. For example, in the iron and steel industry from 1929 to September 1931, man-hours of employment were reduced by more than half, while average hourly earnings fell only 3 percent. The picture was similar in the agricultural implement, automobile, electrical manufacturing, and rubber industries. Reductions in man-hours in these industries ranged from 20 to 80 percent, and hourly earnings fell no more than 3 percent.[2]

If it is true that in a depression many of the unemployed would be willing to work for less than the prevailing wage, why are non-union employers reluctant to cut wages? The answer has at least two parts. The first relates to the specific training the employer has invested in his present workers. In the short run, at least, the unemployed (except perhaps for those the employer has laid off himself) are poor substitutes for the workers he has retained, and he will tend to retain those with the most specific training. The second part of the answer applies even to workers having no specific training, and says that workers universally regard a wage cut as an affront because they view their money wage as a measure of their worth and of the esteem in which they are held. A non-union employer therefore fears that a wage cut will be so resented as to cause a drop in productivity or to encourage the formation of a union. This means that during a depression the employed and the unemployed are essentially noncompeting groups, and the supply price of the unemployed is not relevant to determining the wage level of the employed.

The universal resistance to cuts in money wages, as Keynes emphasized, does not apply with the same force to reductions in the real wage that arise from increases in the prices of consumer goods with money wages constant. This asymmetry in the response to equivalent reductions in real wages in different forms is usually called *money illusion*. Of course, Keynes did not suggest that there is absolute money illusion in the sense that workers or unions would passively accept any and all rises in the price level, no matter how prolonged or severe, without demanding corresponding increases in money wages. But there can be a considerable degree of money illusion in the short run because it takes far longer to perceive price rises than wage cuts, and even when perceived, price rises are much more impersonal and cannot be blamed on the workers' own employer.[3] Furthermore, price increases affect all workers rather uniformly, while money wage cuts take place at different times and in different amounts and therefore involve changes in relative wages.

INCREASES IN THE GENERAL WAGE LEVEL: THE PHILLIPS CURVE

Although the general level of money wages no longer falls in response to an excess supply of labor, it does still rise in response to excess demand. The relation between money wages and unemployment was formalized in an important 1958 article by Professor A. W. Phillips, which introduced what is now called the Phillips curve.[4] A schematic Phillips curve is shown in Figure 24. The variable measured on the vertical axis, $\dot{w}$, is the percentage rate of change of money wages; the horizontal axis shows the unemployment rate, which is used as an (inverted) index of excess demand. The underlying argument is that excess demand will cause money wages to rise, and that the greater the amount of excess demand, the faster the rise. Employers raise money rather than real wages when they are short of labor, because this is the only wage rate under their control; they have no way of lowering the price of consumer goods. Note, however, that money wages cannot adjust instantaneously to excess demand, or the excess demand would never be observed. If an excess of unfilled vacancies over unemployed workers caused an immediate rise in wages to the new equilibrium level, this would imply an immediate increase in the number of workers available for work and an immediate reduction in the number of vacancies employers want to fill, and

FIGURE 24
A Phillips Curve

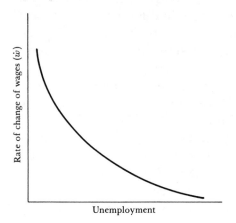

these changes would eliminate the excess demand. Thus the Phillips curve implies that wage adjustments are sluggish, which of course they are.

This mechanism underlying the Phillips curve is shown in Figure 25. In this diagram the vertical axis is the *level* of money wages, not the rate of change as in Figure 24, and the horizontal axis is employment rather than unemployment. If the initial

FIGURE 25
The Generation of the Phillips Curve

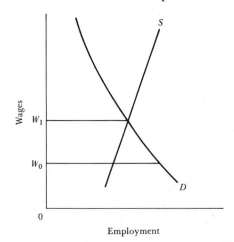

wage were W_0 (because it was an equilibrium wage in an earlier period) and the demand and supply schedules for labor were those shown as D and S, the wage would rise toward W_1. Similarly, if the initial wage were above W_1, wages would fall.

Because the argument underlying the Phillips curve is symmetrical for wage increases and wage decreases, the curve in principle should lie in part below the vertical axis of Figure 24. This was true for the original Phillips curve, which was fitted to British data for the period 1861–1957, during much of which time wages were in fact flexible downward. However, Figure 24 has been drawn to show no negative wage changes and so to reflect the downward wage rigidity of the postwar period. In terms of Figure 25, this assumes that if wages are above W_1, they nevertheless will not fall, and excess supply will persist until the demand or supply schedules shift.

The Phillips curve should in principle be convex as viewed from the origin. Frictional unemployment prevents it from ever reaching the vertical axis, and wages could be expected to rise very rapidly if demand were strong enough to make unemployment lower than normal frictional levels. This makes the curve very steep at the far left. In this region, unemployment is subject to two conflicting influences. The strength of demand reduces the duration of job search for each unemployed worker, since there are many unfilled vacancies. On the other hand, the voluntary quit rate rises, so the number of people frictionally unemployed may rise. We expect the first of these tendencies to outweigh the second; a contrary expectation would produce a Phillips curve with a positive slope.

At the far right, the Phillips curve is flattened by the downward rigidity of money wages. This operates not only for all labor markets taken together, but for each occupational and geographical market separately. The result is that with no wages falling, the average wage will rise to some extent as long as there is excess demand in any submarket, and this may be true even when the aggregate level of unemployment is quite high.

Although the theoretical arguments for expecting convexity in the Phillips curve are strong, a curve does not always fit the data better than a straight line, especially if there are few observations at the extremes. In particular, Phillips curves fitted to American data seldom seem to have any appreciable curvature.

When the Phillips curve is fitted to data, additional variables are usually introduced on the right-hand side of the wage adjustment equation, so that we get something like the following:

$$\dot{w} = a_0 + a_1 u + a_2 \dot{u} + a_3 \dot{p} + e \qquad (1)$$

where $\dot{u}$ is the change in unemployment, $\dot{p}$ is the change in retail prices in the preceding period, and e is an error term. The Phillips curve is then the partial relation between $\dot{w}$ and u (or some transform of u that is nonlinear in the original units) , and changes in $\dot{u}$ and $\dot{p}$ shift the position of the curve. Since these additional variables substantially improve the fit in most cases, they suggest that the actual wage adjustment mechanism involves more than just excess demand. For example, price increases arising from an increased demand for products would eventually move the money demand schedule for labor to the right and would thus generate excess demand for labor. The success of the price-change variable when it is introduced separately suggests that this process has been short-circuited, and prices to some extent (perhaps through collective bargaining) affect wages directly. We shall return to this point in discussing some criticisms of the Phillips curve that focus on the role of price expectations.

The success of the variable $\dot{u}$ means that both the level and the movement of unemployment affect wage changes. Wages rise faster, given the level of unemployment, when unemployment is falling than when it is rising. This variable indicates that employers and unions consider the future as well as the present strength of demand when they are making wage changes. Some estimates substitute a different variable for $\dot{u}$, such as the change in profits. Most such variables measuring changes in broad economic aggregates reflect the phases of the business cycle and they are therefore highly correlated. For this reason it is often hard to choose among them.

WAGE–PRICE RELATIONS
AND POLICY CHOICES

The extraordinary interest of economists and others in the Phillips curve arises from its implications for macroeconomic policy and, in particular, from the linkage between wage changes and price changes. This linkage can be seen most clearly by making some strong assumptions about wage–price relations. We assume first that the rate of change of average productivity (output per man-hour) is constant. This means that for any given wage change there is a single corresponding change in unit labor cost (wages per unit of output). Second, we assume that prices are proportional to unit labor costs, or, in other words, that markups over unit labor cost are a constant proportion of prices. This means that there is a given rate of change in prices corresponding to each rate of change of wages so that the vertical axis of Figure 24 can be transformed from $\dot{w}$ to $\dot{p}$ by a simple shift of scale. For example, with productivity rising at 3 percent, $\dot{w} = 3$ corresponds to $\dot{p} = 0$, and $\dot{w} = 0$ corresponds to $\dot{p} = -3$.

In fact, of course, the linkages are much looser than the preceding paragraph assumes. First, there are both secular and cyclical changes in productivity. Average productivity usually falls when output falls and rises again as output begins to rise, because of the presence of overhead labor and of labor "hoarding" resulting from the fixed costs of employment. These forces are important enough to outweigh the effect of any tendency for workers to be more attentive to their duty when unemployment is high. One can also expect both secular and cyclical changes in markups; the long-term rise in labor's share of national income suggests that markups have fallen secularly, and in competitive markets they fall cyclically when demand is slack.

In its transformed version, with price changes on the vertical axis, the Phillips curve presents the economic policy maker with a menu of choices between two evils he very much wants to avoid: inflation and unemployment. If he chooses a position far to the left, unemployment is close to an irreducible minimum, but the rate of inflation may be unacceptably high; and under fixed rates of exchange between national currencies this may lead to an adverse balance of international payments. If he selects a point farther to the right, inflation is moderated, but at a cost of less than full employment.

Since the terms of trade between employment and inflation often seem unattractive, policy makers attempt to shift the Phillips curve in two ways. First, through an active manpower policy they can attempt to shift the curve to the left. The unemployment measured along the horizontal axis includes frictional and structural unemployment. If these can be reduced by improving the public employment service or by the relocation and retraining of the structurally unemployed, the rate of unemployment corresponding to any given rate of price increase would be reduced. For any given rate of unemployment, there would be fewer unfilled vacancies, and the tendency for wages and prices to rise would be weaker.

Although it has often been pointed out that in principle such policies should shift the Phillips curve, there does not appear to be any evidence that they have in fact succeeded in doing so. Nor would it be desirable to judge the success of manpower policy on this basis, since manpower policies whose benefits greatly exceeded their costs might still fail this severe macroeconomic test.

The second possible method of shifting the Phillips curve is through some kind of incomes policy or wage–price guideposts. These policies, if successful, should lower the rates of wage and price increases associated with a given level of unemployment and thus should shift the Phillips curve downward. This possibility will be discussed further at the end of the chapter.

EXPECTATIONS AND
THE LONG-RUN PHILLIPS CURVE

Recently some economists have begun to question whether the Phillips curve does in fact show the choices confronting policy makers. They argue that the Phillips curve we observe is one traced out historically when people never knew what rate of change of prices to expect. If policy makers were able to hold the economy at one particular point on the curve, everyone would come to expect the rate of inflation associated with this particular point. These expectations would cause people to change their behavior. Unions would demand wage gains larger than the expected rate of price increase. Employers seeking to recruit labor would have to raise their wages by more than the expected increase in the wages of their competitors in the labor market. These behavioral changes would produce a new long-run Phillips curve steeper than the historical one.[5]

In much of what I shall call the "expectations literature," it is argued that the long-run Phillips curve is vertical; that when enough time has passed to permit the complete adjustment of expectations to the constant rate of price change chosen by policy makers, the rate of unemployment will be the same whatever rate of price change has been selected. This so-called natural rate of unemployment is uniquely determined by the structure of the labor market.

This version of the expectations argument seems to be correct in only two cases: when there is extremely rapid price change (hyperinflation) or when it is virtually costless to make wage changes. In other circumstances, lags in the wage-adjustment process will still give the long-run Phillips curve a negative slope, though a steeper one than that of the historical Phillips curve. Although wages may be inappropriately low given employer expectations, the employers will balance the gains from raising them (improved recruitment) against the costs. In fact, employers and even unions behave as though wage adjustments were very costly, perhaps in part because every change in wage levels threatens to reopen many vexing problems of wage structure. For example, if it is agreed that the wages of several different skills or crafts should be increased, should they rise by the same percentage, by the same dollar amount, or by something in between? For obvious reasons, the best-paid crafts will prefer the percentage increase and the lowest-paid will prefer the same dollar amount.[6]

WAGE-PUSH INFLATION

It is possible to explain the shape of the Phillips curve without any reference to excess demand or the bidding-up of wages by employers. Suppose that trade unions are strong enough and aggressive enough to win wage increases even when there is excess supply, but that they are more aggressive when unemployment is relatively low than when it is very high. Such behavior could generate a curve like the Phillips curve even though there was never any excess demand in any market.

The excess-demand explanation of wage increases underlying the Phillips curve suggests that money wages rise because of demand pull. In the bargaining-power explanation just suggested as an alternative, the rise in money wages is initiated by trade unions, at least to the extent that the wage increase exceeds the rise in productivity. Most economists would agree that both mechanisms operate at times, with the balance between them differing in different countries and circumstances. The purest forms of demand inflation occur in wartime when there are enormous excess demands for goods and labor. Under these circumstances collective-bargaining agreements, with their fixed durations, can retard the adjustment of money wages, and union–nonunion wage differentials may be compressed. On the other hand, wage increases during periods of substantial unemployment are best explained by the bargaining-power, or *wage-push*, model.

Countries differ in the extent to which an increase in union wages could be expected to lead to a general rise in the level of money wages. Where the unionized sector is small and the threat of union expansion into unorganized sectors is weak, the principal effect of wage increases in the union sector will be on the pattern of relative wages. The general level of wages will be little affected by union gains. However, wage increases will be larger in the unionized sector and smaller in the nonunion sector (because of increased labor supply) than they would have been in the absence of unions. The growth of employment in the union sector will be discouraged by these widening differentials between union and nonunion wages, while the growth of employment in the non-union sector will be encouraged. This pattern seems to fit the experience of the United States during the 1950s.[7]

Eventually, however, the increasing wage differentials must stabilize, in part because the employment effects of the differentials will tend to inhibit further wage gains in the union sector, and in part because the widening differentials will encourage previously unorganized groups to become organized in unions or professional associations. The first effect weakens the wage push; the second, however, makes it become more general.

The greater the extent of union organization, and the greater the threat that collective bargaining will spread to groups in the economy whose wages and salaries have not previously been set by negotiation, the more likely are union pressures to raise the general level of money wages rather than to affect only relative wages. When most workers are organized or subject to a credible threat of organization, a rise in the general wage level can originate in collective bargaining, perhaps in a fairly small part of the union sector, and then spread by emulation or *coercive comparison* to other industries or occupations. The larger the wage increases won by unions, the more wages nonunion employers will have to offer their own workers if they hope to remain unorganized.

The experience of the United States in 1970–1971 seems to illustrate some of the symptoms of wage-push inflation. An upward movement of wages that began in the late 1960s was originally caused by excess demand growing out of the Vietnam War and the way it was financed. By mid-1969, however, output had peaked and the economy entered a mild but rather long recession. By late 1970 unemployment was well above frictional levels. Wages kept on increasing, however, as unions whose contracts expired sought to match the gains other unions had won when demand was stronger. If observations for 1970 and 1971 are plotted against a Phillips curve fitted to data for earlier years, they lie well above the old curve.

One factor in the unusual experience of 1970–1971 may well be the extension of unionization to new sectors of the economy. During this period there was a rapid spread of collective bargaining to the public sector of the economy and a new militance and willingness to strike appeared among public-employee unions. Similarly, unionism spread to such previously unorganized employers as nonprofit hospitals and private universities. This growth of collective bargaining posed further threats to employers in sectors as yet unreached.

It is possible to combine the excess-demand model of wage adjustment with a wage-push model in a single estimating equation that includes both unemployment and unionism variables. The unionism effect can be represented by changes in membership, by number of strikes, or by bargaining elections won. Thus one could have an equation like

$$\dot{w} = a_o + a_1 u + a_2 \dot{p} + a_3 m + e \tag{2}$$

where m is the number of union members and the other symbols are the same as in equation (1) above. Several models of this sort have been estimated with the general result that more of the variation in money wages is explained when the unionism variable is included, but the effect of unemployment becomes much weaker.[8]

INCOMES POLICY

Governments seeking to restrain wage-push inflation have two main choices, neither of them very appealing. First, they can allow the rate of unemployment to increase by refusing to create enough aggregate demand to absorb the old level of output at the new level of wages and prices. This policy is sometimes called refusing to *validate* the wage increase. In fact, the policy does nothing to roll back the wage increases already negotiated, but it may lengthen the period until the next round of increases or reduce their size when they come. This is in essence the policy pursued in the United States in 1970.

The alternative is to attempt to limit wage and price increases directly, through wage and price controls or related policies. Such policies can take a variety of forms. For short periods, they can involve a wage freeze or wage pause during which no increases in money wages are permitted. Wage freezes are most used in wartime or during a balance-of-payments crisis. Thus the U.S. wage–price freeze of August 1971 was announced in connection with measures designed to improve the international balance of payments. For the longer term, most policies seek to establish some guideposts or criteria for acceptable increases in money wages. These are usually based on the trend of average productivity, sometimes with larger increases permitted where output is increased by the increased skill or effort of the workers concerned, as in British productivity bargaining. Special provisions are often made for cases of equity—those of low-wage workers or workers whose wages have lagged behind those of other comparable workers. When there is already an ongoing inflation, the wage criterion may be adjusted upward to allow for it. This explains the difference between the 1960s' U.S. wage guideposts of 3.2 percent and the 1971–1972 pay standard of 5.5 percent.

Incomes policy can be administered by a government agency; by a tripartite agency including union, management, and public representatives; or by unions and management themselves without active government participation, as in Sweden. Most incomes policies have the force of law, but some, such as the U.S. wage–price guideposts of 1962–1966, have relied instead on exhortation and informal government pressures.

The record of incomes policies to date includes few if any cases in which increases in money wages have been successfully restrained over long periods. In some cases this is because they were not accompanied by monetary and fiscal policies that contributed to restraining inflation.

Incomes policies tend to break down for different reasons under different kinds of institutions. Where there is a highly centralized trade-union movement committed to an incomes policy, as in Sweden, the principal threat to the policy is *wage drift*, which occurs when actual money earnings rise faster than the basic wage rates negotiated in national agreements. In part, wage drift arises because individual employers offer to particular groups of workers in short supply wage increases larger than those negotiated nationally. If such behavior is disapproved or regulated, employers may increase workers' earnings by scheduling additional overtime work, some of which adds little or nothing to output. Employers may also upgrade, or hire, workers into job classifications above those for which they are qualified.

Wage drift is a particularly serious problem under some kinds of piecework or incentive-pay systems. Small improvements in methods can cumulatively increase output per man-hour with the result that earnings rise for any given amount of work effort. When labor is not scarce, management usually attempts to recapture some of such extra earnings by negotiating changes in the piecework rates, perhaps after new industrial engineering studies. When labor is in short supply, however, management may accept the high earnings as an aid to recruitment. Eventually such "methods drift" causes unrest among workers on time rates, who see less skilled pieceworkers earning more than they do. In some British industries this has led to special additional payments to time workers in lieu of the opportunity for high piecework earnings. Wage drift has never been an important phenomenon in the United States, but it has been in many European countries.

In countries where the trade unions do not accept incomes policies or are highly decentralized, so that strikes for higher wages are initiated by national unions in particular industries, by local unions, or even by shop stewards or small groups of workers, wage drift is no longer the main weakness of incomes policy. The most important problem becomes the settlement of strikes in which demands far exceed those permitted by the wage criteria or guideposts. The economic program of the government comes in conflict with the right to strike and with the political costs, to the government in power, of taking strong action against unions. In both the United States and the United Kingdom important wage settlements in excess of the criteria of incomes policy have been permitted to go unchallenged or have been allowed to stand over initial government objections. If this happens frequently, then incomes policy loses its credibility and must be either discarded or revamped.

It should not be assumed, however, that union leaders will always be unwilling to cooperate in efforts to restrain negotiated wage increases in peacetime. A counterexample is furnished by the Construction Industry Stabilization Committee in the United States, established in March 1971. This continued as a tripartite organization with the active participation of national union presidents even after union leaders from the AFL-CIO had resigned from the Pay Board, which regulated wages in other industries. During 1971–1972 the Construction Industry Stabilization Committee substantially slowed the rate of increase of construction wages and fringe benefits. The continued cooperation of national union leaders appears to have been based on their realization that large wage gains won by powerful local unions were in some cases posing threats to the maintenance of employment in the union sector of the industry.

Even where incomes policies do not have a visible effect on wage changes, they may serve other purposes. In several European countries with incomes policies, the rate of increase in money wages in recent years has been above 8 percent per annum—at least double the increase in output per man-hour.[9] It may well be wondered what purpose is served by an incomes policy that permits wage increases of this size. Perhaps the answer is that it is politically impossible for a government to choose a position this far to the left along the Phillips curve without at least giving the appearance of combatting the resulting inflation. The incomes policy is then the political price of considering inflation rather than unemployment as the lesser of the avoidable evils. Alternatively, the answer could be that without an incomes policy the rise in wages would have been even more rapid.

Shortly after World War II, Charles O. Hardy stated that it is impossible to have simultaneously full employment, stable prices, and strong trade unions. He argued that one could have any pair of these three, but not all three. Twenty-five years later, after much discussion and effort, the dilemma seems no less serious. Perhaps future developments in labor economics will offer some additional guidance on the extent to which we should choose somewhat more unemployment than the frictional level, some continual upward drift of the price level, or some stronger restraints on the power of unions to negotiate wage increases without interference. As unemployment was the great economic problem of the interwar period, rises in the general price and wage level have been the great problem of the postwar period, though by no means so costly a problem. But there has not yet been a general theory of the wage and price level that fully integrates the older monetary theories of inflation with the changed institutional patterns of the postwar world.

NOTES

1. J. M. Keynes, *The General Theory of Employment, Interest, and Money* (London: Macmillan, 1936) , chap. 19.
2. See A. Rees, "Wage Determination and Involuntary Unemployment," *Journal of Political Economy* 59 (April 1951) , 143–153.
3. For statistical evidence of the presence of short-run money illusion in consumption behavior, see W. H. Branson and A. K. Klevorick, "Money Illusion and the Aggregate Consumption Function," *American Economic Review* 59 (December 1969) , 832–849.
4. A. W. Phillips, "The Relation Between Unemployment and the Rate of Change of Money Wage Rates in the United Kingdom, 1861–1957," *Economica* (November 1958) .
5. For a brief version of this argument, see Milton Friedman, "The Role of Monetary Policy," *American Economic Review* 58 (March 1968), 1–17. For a more technical version, see E. S. Phelps, "Money-Wage Dynamics and Labor Market Equilibrium," *Journal of Political Economy* 76 (July–August 1968) , 678–711.
6. For an extended version of the argument of this paragraph, see A. Rees, "The Phillips Curve as a Menu for Policy Choice," *Economica* (August 1970) .
7. See A. W. Throop, "The Union Non-union Wage Differential and Cost-Push Inflation," *American Economic Review* (March 1968) .
8. For an early model of this type, see A. G. Hines, "Trade Unions and Wage Inflation in the United Kingdom, 1893–1961," *Review of Economic Studies* 31 (1964) , 221–251. For a similar study using American data, see O. C. Ashenfelter, G. E. Johnson, and J. Pencavel, "Trade Unions and the Rate of Change of Money Wages in the United States," *Review of Economic Studies* 39 (January 1972) , 27–54.
9. See *On Incomes Policy*, Papers and Proceedings from a conference in honor of Erik Lundberg (Stockholm: The Industrial Council for Social and Economic Studies, 1969) , p. 309, especially the data for Norway, Sweden, Denmark, and the Netherlands.

243